LIVING WITH HEROIN

Living with Heroin

The impact of a drugs 'epidemic'
on an English community

Howard Parker, Keith Bakx and Russell Newcombe

Open University Press
Milton Keynes • Philadelphia

Open University Press
Open University Educational Enterprises Limited
12 Cofferidge Close
Stony Stratford
Milton Keynes MK11 1BY

and
242 Cherry Street
Philadelphia, PA 19106, USA

First published 1988

Copyright © 1988 Howard Parker, Keith Bakx and Russell Newcombe

British Library Cataloguing in Publication Data

Parker, Howard
  Living with heroin : the impact of a drugs
  'epidemic' on an English community.
  1. Heroin habit — Great Britain
  I. Title II. Bakx, Keith III. Newcombe, Russell
  362.2'93'0941   HV5822.H4

  ISBN 0–335–15565–0
  ISBN 0–335–15564–2 Pbk

Library of Congress Cataloging-in-Publication Data

Parker, Howard J.
  Living with heroin : the impact of a drugs
  'epidemic' on an English community.
  Bibliography: p.
  Includes index.
  1. Heroin habit — England — Wirral (Merseyside)
  2. Heroin habit — England — Wirral (Merseyside) — Prevention
  I. Bakx, Keith II. Newcombe, Russell III. Title
  HV5822.H4P37 1988 362.2 932 094275 87–31327

  ISBN 0–335–15565–0   ISBN 0–335–15564–2 (pbk.)

Typeset by Burns & Smith, Derby.
Printed in Great Britain by Redwood Burn Ltd.

Contents

Acknowledgements

We would like to thank the following individuals and organisations for their co-operation and help: Tina Benson, Carolyne Butt, Cherie Chadwick, Pat Fleming, Richard Hartnoll, Graham Jarvis, John Marks, Chris Mills, Joy Mott, Pat O'Hare, Pauline Olsen, Allan Parry, Maggie Pearson, Geoff Pearson, Ken Pease, Martin Plant, John Strang, Carol Williams. Arrowe Park Hospital and Detoxification Unit, The Department of Environment, Liverpool Drug Dependency Unit, Mersey Regional Alcohol and Drug Dependency Unit, Mersey Regional Drug Training and Information Centre, Merseyside Drugs Council, Merseyside Police, Merseyside Probation Service, Society for Biophysical Medicine. Wirral Committee for Solvent Abuse, Wirral's Social Services (Housing, Education, Planning and Estates Departments), Wirral Medical Committee, Family Practitioners Committee and Wirral GPs. Wirral District Health Authority, Home Office Drugs Branch, and the Coroner for Wirral.

We especially thank Wirral heroin users and their families, as well as the several hundred school pupils, college students and YTS trainees and apprentices who helped with our study.

Glossary of terms used in the text

acid	*d*-lysergic acid diethylamide (LSD)
bag	smallest amount of heroin bought or sold, enough for between one and three 'hits'; also called a 'wrap'
barbs	barbiturates, e.g., Tuinal, Nembutal
bizzies	the police
breadhead	anyone who places a high value on money, but especially a heroin dealer who does not use heroin him/herself
bust	arrest and/or search by police for drugs
chasing the dragon	heating heroin on aluminium foil and inhaling the fumes through a funnel such as an empty biro tube
clonidine	drug generally prescribed for high blood pressure, but also given to heroin users to relieve withdrawal symptoms
cranking	injecting
cut	mixed with dilutant such as glucose
dabble	use a drug on an occasional or irregular basis
dealer	retailer of illegal drugs
DF118s	dihydrocodeine, a synthetic opioid used as a mild painkiller
diamorphine	heroin
Diconal	a moderate to severe painkiller containing synthetic opioids
dikes	Diconal
draw	cannabis
drop-out	generally an individual who does not share the same set of social values as society 'at large'
drought	a severe shortage of an illegal drug
fix	inject

foil	aluminium foil used in the process of 'chasing the dragon'
gear	illegal drugs, especially heroin
habit	dependent use of drugs; addiction
hassle	(cause) difficulties
high, hit	intoxication through drug use
hooked	addicted, dependent, habituated
joint	a hand-rolled cigarette containing cannabis and, usually, tobacco
junkie	heroin addict; person dependent upon heroin
methadone	synthetic opioid used as a substitute for heroin in treatment programmes
mong out	state of drowsiness/euphoria resulting from opioid use
mushies	hallucinogenic fungi, e.g., psilocybe
nod	see 'mong out'
Omnopon	an opium preparation
Palfium	an opioid used as a moderate to severe painkiller
Palfs	Palfium
pinkies	Diconal
plod	police officer
pot	cannabis
rip off	to overcharge, defraud or steal
score	to purchase drugs
script	a prescription for drugs
skag	heroin
smack	heroin
smackhead	heroin user
snort	to take (generally) powdered drug by sniffing
speed	any stimulant drug, but especially amphetamines
stoned	intoxicated
strung out	experiencing withdrawal symptoms
toot	the act of inhaling or sniffing a drug, especially heroin or cocaine
Tuinal	a barbiturate
turkey	withdrawal symptoms
turn on	to introduce someone to an intoxicating drug
works	equipment needed for injecting
wrap	a small quantity of heroin, also 'bag'

Introduction

This is a story, albeit a social scientific one, about what happened to a community in the North-West of England when, suddenly and unexpectedly, within the course of about three years, several thousand of its younger and poorest residents became regular heroin users. This is not a tidy tale, though, for as yet it has no ending: heroin use remains prevalent and its meaning and consequences continue to multiply. However, the significance of this heroin 'outbreak' is such that it needs to be reported now. Consequently our primary aim, in writing this book, is to provide an up-to-date, empirical study which looks at the new heroin users of the 1980s and the impact of their developing lifestyle on themselves, their families and their community.

A successful story needs more than description and observation, however, it needs a structure and coherence which tells the reader not only what is happening, but why. In the non-fictional world of social science this usually means developing a coherent conceptual and theoretical perspective. This has not been easy to construct. Surprisingly British sociology and criminology, routinely adept at providing such frameworks, have not been instantly helpful on this occasion. Studies of drug misuse conducted during the 1970s tended to focus on middle-class cannabis use, accurately portrayed as victimless. Societal overreaction was also documented in relation to the 'moral panics' of adults coping with youthful deviance and the social 'misconstruction', and thus mismanagement, of subcultural responses by working-class youth. Whilst we will describe extensive official mismanagement in relation to heroin use (Chapters 4, 5, 7 and 9), the sociological literature is less helpful in explaining the role and significance of heroin for new working-class users of both sexes. Nor can this community's heroin 'problem' be regarded simply as the product of a moral panic.

If the sociological literature needs some nursing, the medical literature needs intensive care. The endless series of reports based on the clinic populations of 'addicts' treated by psychiatrists and others, which have filled the pages of journals like the *British Journal of Addiction*, describe a group of drug users very different from the subjects of our study. There is very little in this literature for a community-based case study to recognise and embrace.

This is not to criticise either the sociological or medical perspectives on opioid use. What we are identifying here is a credibility gap between our society's 1970s knowledge base and the mercurial arrival of heroin use within a young urban working-class population of the 1980s. It is in this uncomfortable space that we must write and try to locate conceptual and theoretical perspectives which make sense of our data. In the end we have found that the American literature, not usually a productive source of explanation for British social phenomena, offers the few conceptual supports which do not collapse under our data. Moreover, it is the Americans' willingness to combine medical and sociological perspectives when explaining widespread heroin use in their inner cities, which offers most. In particular a batch of epidemiological studies of heroin outbreaks or 'epidemics', set alongside parallel sociological explanations of the role of drugs subcultures and the alternative economy, have proved vital.

Such cannibalisation must only be a temporary measure, however, to shore up what understanding we have until more substantive theory, sensitive to the British scene, is built. We do not attempt this construction, though our struggle to make sense of the scale and potency of heroin use in this English community will hopefully stimulate others so to do. What we do claim is that the appropriate explanatory framework will not emerge from one discipline or from one case study.

Chapter 1 provides a brief history of the first phase of official responses to heroin use in Wirral, Merseyside, the community in question. It looks at the role of the media and concerned local people in defining heroin 'abuse' as a public and consequently political problem. It also outlines how an initial official response was shaped by local politicians and a plethora of local professionals into a manageable form. The three strands of this 'first-phase' strategy were *prevention* through education in schools, *control* via saturation policing, and *treatment* through detoxification and counselling schemes. The failure of this strategy is documented throughout the book.

Chapter 2 reports on the results of a major survey of 'known' drug takers using the recording systems of ten key local agencies. It offers a detailed profile of the new heroin users, showing just how different in terms of age, gender, social and economic status and personal circumstances they are from known '1970s' users. Chapter 3 both reconstructs the history of Wirral's heroin 'epidemic' between 1979 and 1986 and, via the results of a second survey, produces a forecast of how the prevalence and incidence of heroin use will develop in Wirral. This exercise, although it involves us in a critical review of the modelling of heroin 'epidemics', does show that epidemiology has a contribution to make in understanding the spread of heroin use in this particular community.

Our analysis of the 'known' sector of heroin use continues in Chapter 4, where we report the findings of in-depth interviews with 61 regular users. Their motivational accounts and reported drugs careers allow us to build up a more complete picture of how their heroin use began via social processes in their immediate community. Our respondents discuss their feelings about the drug and how becoming dependent upon it has affected their lives. They also provide a consumers' view of detoxification and counselling services.

In Chapter 5 we continue to employ qualitative research methods and describe a technique, called 'snowballing', for interviewing 'hidden' drug users, that is, those not known to official agencies. On the basis of snowballing four different user networks we obtained interviews with over 60 regular heroin takers. This allowed us to compare the social characteristics of both the 'hidden' and 'known' sectors. We found, for instance, that middle-class and female users were more likely to remain hidden. Based on our snowballs we were also able to produce an estimate of Wirral's overall regular heroin-using population, which proved to be twice the size of the known sector.

Chapter 6 is taken up by four detailed case studies of persons for whom heroin has been a central part of their recent lives. Using their own words, these four people describe their experiences of living with (and without) heroin.

Chapter 7 begins by detailing the unprecedented rise in recorded crime which has beset Wirral since 1981. It goes on to explore how this crime wave is related to the area's heroin-using population, based on analysis of both official records and self-reported offending described by regular users. The picture we paint, whilst unfinished, bears remarkable similarities to portraits of American inner cities where heroin use, drug distribution networks, acquisitive crime and dangerous lifestyles intertwine and develop despite heavy policing and stiff sentencing.

In Chapter 8 we survey the alcohol, tobacco and illicit drug use of a sample of Wirral's 'ordinary' young people: schoolchildren, college students and those on a youth employment scheme. Their widespread use of alcohol, tobacco and cannabis, their attitudes to drugs and the significance of their friends' behaviour are used both as a predictor of continuing drugs careers and as a context in which to understand heroin better. This context is very different from the one created by the media and central government's 'war' on drugs. It needs to be, for in Chapter 9 we consider how, if 'Heroin Screws You Up', misunderstanding *why* it does so 'screws up' those charged with society's official responses. Chapter 9 documents how local officials in Wirral, perplexed by the failure of their prevention–control–treatment strategy, talked themselves into a kind of collective paralysis, whereby they could not agree on the components of any revised 'second-phase' response. We try to isolate the sources of their disagreements and identify the very real dilemmas they must face on behalf of their community. Dealing with the unwanted side effects of such widespread heroin use, be they the plight of users and their families, the spread of AIDS or the victims of crime, has weighed heavily on these local decision-makers. They have not yet learnt how to live with heroin.

1

Smack in the middle

Wirral

Most working-class Merseysiders can be easily recognised from their accent and dialect, referred to as 'scouse'. There are many jokes in scouse humour about Wirral. Nearly all these refer to Wirral residents' apparent belief that they are socially and economically superior to those across the River Mersey in Liverpool. Thus, on the Liverpool side, Wirral people are referred to as 'the stuck-up nobodies across the water' and worse. Liverpool is, in turn, blamed by Wirralians for bringing and spreading all manner of evil across the whole region.

Wirral is a predominantly white community of about 340,000 people fairly tightly packed onto a peninsula separated from Wales by the River Dee and, as we have said, from Liverpool by the River Mersey. The barely submerged class antagonism much alluded to in the local humour is both true and false. It is true because Wirral, as a suburban borough with an interesting and extensive coastline, an impressive green belt, some extremely affluent townships, a large number of owner-occupiers and a thriving private schools sector, does have the look and feel of a very well-heeled community. It is false because Wirral also has, in very close proximity to its affluent townships, a large and very poor 'redundant' working-class population. The borough's numerous municipal housing estates and legacy of dockland neighbourhoods house people suffering from levels of deprivation and unemployment as severe as anywhere in the United Kingdom. In the absence of a memorable quotation from a famous person startled by this contrast, we are compelled to suggest that Wirral is, in many respects, a microcosm of a 'two nations' contemporary England. It has its very own North–South divide, with the axes of housing, schooling, employment, and consequently wealth, class and politics all reliably reflecting this division.

The making of the heroin problem

We can now see that it all began in 1979. At first things developed largely unnoticed with new heroin-user networks establishing in Woodchurch, Ford and Moreton. By the end of 1981 and into 1982, however, these new outbreaks were occurring with a rapidity and density which in retrospect can be seen as the building blocks for a full-blown heroin 'epidemic'. These foundations were laid in the deprived urban areas of the community — smack in the middle of Wirral.

Even at the end of 1981 very few people in Wirral had any inkling that the area would, within two years, be alleged to have one of the largest heroin 'problems' in the United Kingdom. Nor would they have expected their community's problem to become the focus of one of the most intensive and long-lasting media campaigns the borough has experienced.

In this opening chapter, we describe very briefly how local politicians and statutory and voluntary services first responded to the emerging heroin outbreaks in the 1982–5 period. (The second phase of official responses is discussed in Chapter 9.) We should remember that, like so many other British communities outside London, Wirral entered the 1980s with no more than a handful of long-term drug users known to local doctors. The borough had no specific structures for discussing drug misuse and the local authority had no statutory responsibilities for dealing with any unwanted consequences. Indeed, Wirral had no more reason to have such structures than it had for setting up multi-professional committees to discuss the dangers of residents keeping snakes as pets in council-owned properties.

There was, therefore, no real chance of this community predicting the scale of the problem, and no prospect of the early signs of widespread heroin use being fully appreciated. Earlier experiences in England were long forgotten (de Alceron 1969) and no connections with the hard-learnt American experiences were made. Consequently, Wirral, along with a handful of other British urban communities, has during the 1980s been hit by heroin about as heavily as a community can. Wirral's heroin 'epidemic' 'incubated' unnoticed and in documenting this fact we can do no better than quote an epidemiologist (Hughes 1977) working within a similar heroin outbreak in Chicago during the early 1960s: 'In this epidemic there was a tragic time lag between the contagious stage during which heroin use spread and the stage when the epidemic's full impact was felt and reacted to by the host community.'

Ironically it was during the very period that heroin was covertly establishing a hold in the community that concern about adolescents misusing solvents was the subject of official response. The increased misuse of solvents had been brought to Wirral Council's attention by the Chief Constable of Merseyside in December 1982. Police concern was soon matched by that of voluntary sector workers and the schools. Subsequently, after a series of meetings initiated by the then Director of Social Services, the Wirral Committee on Solvent Abuse was set up. Although rather overshadowed by the heroin 'problem' which soon emerged, this committee was able to continue its focus on young solvent users and obtained funding for a full-time counsellor to work out of a Council of Voluntary Service office.

Evidence of widespread heroin use in the community built up rapidly during 1983–4. It came from a number of sources, but without doubt the media played a key role in making heroin a suitable enemy. In 1983–4, Wirral not only made the headlines in the tabloid newspapers, but fast became the place for the in-depth story. Thus, during 1984, investigative journalism had a field day. Birkenhead, Wirral's principal town, was dubbed 'Smack City' by *The Observer* and apocryphal stories about heroin in school dinners and £5 wraps in ice-cream cornets on sale outside primary schools, first constructed in the popular Press, soon found their way into the worthy *Times Educational Supplement* (9 March 1984). Three major national television documentaries, including one on the work of the local Drugs Squad, brought Wirral to national attention. Wirral was portrayed as being a community in a state of shock caught up in a problem for which it had no explanations or obvious solution.

Even when the story was out of the national news, the regional media, now well connected to useful sources, kept it rolling. Local radio claimed that 50 per cent of young people between 14 and 25 were using heroin regularly. Local newspapers ran campaigns focusing on what needed to be done at a grass roots level and the region's evening paper, the *Liverpool Echo*, mounted an unprecedented campaign, culminating in its 'Drugs: A Generation in Peril' series during September 1984. Once again Wirral was singled out with headlines about many babies being born addicted to heroin in Wirral's maternity units and moving stories about local families wrecked by heroin addiction. A summary of the *Echo*'s series was distributed to all political parties' autumn conferences and indeed mentioned in Parliament.

Initially, journalists obtained most of their stories from concerned people in the townships where heroin was concentrated. Several local pressure groups were emerging during this period, demanding from their MPs and councillors that something be done. One group, Parents Against Drug Abuse (PADA), was particularly influential and achieved very considerable regional and national media attention in its efforts to gain help and resources. This partnership, whereby demands from affected families were willingly publicised by the media, produced a keen atmosphere and put very considerable pressure on politicians and local authority professionals. It was, sadly, to be the first and last major impact of the parents' movement during the initial phase of responses.

Against this backcloth, the first phase was taking shape, and in October 1983 the problem of heroin use was raised in the local Council, initially in the Education Committee and subsequently in the main Policy and Resources Committee. The Council decided to take the initiative. It invited various statutory and voluntary organisations to take part in a co-ordinating committee to study the problem and consider what action was required in terms of publicity, health education and the co-ordination of agency responses. It was only at this stage, when representatives from different professional and administrative structures began to be consulted, that official worry and concern about the scale of heroin use began to take shape.

Much information was eventually to emerge from medical sources. However, in 1983–4, the only readily available message was that GPs were referring an unusually large number of patients with drugs problems to the two local psychiatric departments and the Regional Alcohol and Drug Dependency Unit (as our analysis of case files later showed). One of the local psychiatrists, appreciating the scale of the problem, applied to the District Health Authority for resources to open a detoxification clinic. His request was initially shelved, but then taken up when new money was made available from the DHSS 'initiative' to open up treatment facilities for drug users nationally.

The significance and scale of the surge of patients to GPs was in most other respects not appreciated. Only in retrospect, after our detailed research, did it become clear to anyone what had transpired in GPs' surgeries throughout Wirral in 1982–4. For whilst the Family Practitioners' Committee had met in early 1983 to discuss the heroin issue, they were primarily concerned with the pressures on doctors and so kept their worries to themselves. The 'intelligence', which was in theory available by collating the experiences of local family doctors, remained undiscovered or privatised. Similarly, although Wirral GPs notified an exceptionally large number of drug addicts to the Home Office during 1983, the significance of this was not quickly identified even by regional Drugs Branch. The Home Office Drugs Branch has shown itself hopelessly ineffective at quickly and effectively using the Notifications Index to warn and inform local communities about extensive drug use. And so it was for Wirral, for, as we shall see in Chapter 2, the Index was collecting 'epidemic' data but its guardians did not recognise or communicate the fact.

During this same period the local police, courts and probation service were noting a rapid increase in offences involving the possession and supply of drugs and, more subtly, in the number of crimes involving offenders said to be or admitting to be heroin users. Again it was quite some time before the connections were made and this information was fed into the collective consciousness of local government.

Developing official responses

The Council's initiative to set up a multi-professional group to address the borough's drugs problem was well conceived for it allowed, for the first time, the information and concerns picked up by various parties in relation to heroin to be pulled together. Made up of senior management representatives of key departments like the police, education, hospitals, GPs, probation services, social services, Drugs Branch, the voluntary agencies and local councillors, the Wirral Drug Abuse Committee emerged in late 1983. It formed the basis of the first phase of the community's official response to heroin, although, as we shall see in Chapter 9, its creation in the local government rather than regional health structure was unfortunate.

In January 1984, the Drug Abuse Committee and Wirral Council began their work in earnest. Information offered by the Committee's membership proved substantial enough to suggest something unprecedented was occurring in the borough, but not accurate enough to remove uncertainty and speculation about the size of the heroin problem. The need for research was thus recognised.

A ten-point plan emerged during the spring of 1984. Some items were of little more than symbolic significance, but others were more substantial. Perhaps the single most important decision was to set up a Wirral-wide counselling service for drug users. Because Wirral, as an urban borough with areas of high social need, was eligible for additional central funds from the Department of Environment's Inner Area Programme, it was able to allocate funds rapidly to finance this. Consequently the new Drugs Counselling service, with six counsellors, initially funded for three years, got under way in July 1984. In conjunction with the opening of the new Detoxification Clinic, this seemed to be a good beginning.

The Education Department also moved quickly from November 1983, having had a particularly bumpy ride at the hands of the media. Meetings were held with all secondary school headteachers to discuss the drugs problem and a video was made to facilitate in-service training for teachers. Parents' meetings were held in all 26 secondary schools and special emphasis on drugs work was accepted by the Youth Service. By 1985, the development of a preventive health education package for junior school (nine to 11 years) children was almost complete and a similar scheme for secondary school (11–17 years) children was in the making.

Other plans initiated during 1984 were longer in coming to fruition and one idea, to open a short stay 'crash pad' for users in crisis, was dropped altogether. A parents' advice centre with a shop-front, which PADA asked the Council to provide, was nearly 18 months in getting under way. The delay was partly due to a long and very public debate between PADA and ARROW, a group of residents from Woodchurch, the estate where heroin use was first discovered, who were unhappy about such a centre being opened near their homes, fearing it would attract various sorts of trouble.

Proposals for two new residential establishments were made in 1984. One involved a small unit in the form of a bedsit-type hostel with facilities for 14 residents. This was opened in 1986 under the auspices of the Drugs Council and a local housing trust. The second proposal was to set up a long-term residential therapeutic centre which eventually involved inviting Phoenix House, an established and reputable charity, to set up in Wirral. However, for funding reasons this centre was to be for the whole region. Numerous delays prevented this venture coming to fruition within the 'initial responses' period. During 1985, the Apex Trust, in conjunction with the Manpower Services Commission, and helped by the Council through the Inner Area Programme, set up a training project for local unemployed ex-offenders with a view to helping their job prospects. Many of these trainees had a drugs problem.

The Council's ten-point plan also included approaching Customs and Excise with exhortations about increased searches for illicit supplies and also involved a delegation going to the Home Office to meet the minister concerned with drug misuse. The Chief Constable was also asked to launch a major operation in Wirral to crack down on suppliers. This in fact occurred between mid-1984 and early 1985, with several hundred people being prosecuted for Misuse of Drugs Act offences and acquisitive crime related to their drug dependency. Furthermore, a temporary local heroin drought was created in the borough. However, as we shall see, the enormous ramifications of this draconian approach by the police were not always as intended.

The plan of the Drug Abuse Committee and the Council also involved the commissioning of the research investigation upon which this book is based. The Council suggested the need for independent 'unified' research to ascertain the size and scope of the heroin problem, as they feared that otherwise a number of 'in-house' research papers would be produced which would lack co-ordination and the necessary overview. After various negotiations between government departments, Wirral Council and Liverpool University, the Misuse of Drugs Research Project began in May 1985. Our brief extended beyond looking at the prevalence of heroin use and included documenting the impact of the 'epidemic' on the local community, evaluating service provision and recommending and updating a strategy for dealing with the negative effects of widespread heroin use.

On the face of it, these early responses look most impressive: firm control of those involved in supplying and possessing drugs, an effort in the schools to dissuade young people from experimenting with drugs, and, finally, treatment and counselling facilities to help current users cope with this situation and eventually overcome their dependency. Indeed, putting together such a wide-reaching programme so rapidly was only possible because of the high degree of inter-agency co-operation and commitment by local politicians, officers and professionals. It is the fact that Wirral's heroin 'epidemic' has continued despite these not inconsiderable official efforts that makes the writing of this book important for, as we shall see, this community's heroin problem still resists official antidotes.

2

Counting heads: estimating prevalence and profiling the heroin user

The most noticeable deficit in the 1980s debate about drug use in the UK is the almost complete lack of accurate information about how many people are using illicit drugs. Consequently, there is a constant sense of unreality about much of the policy discussion and a continued credibility gap between academic theory about drugs and the reality of drug use. Thus, although the main aim of our research was to help Wirral Council to develop policies and plan services for heroin users, based on a sound empirical base, we also had an eye to improving methods of estimating prevalence which any community might employ to answer such questions as: How many residents are known to use heroin or other illicit drugs? Which areas are most affected? Which sections of the community are most likely to try heroin or become regular users? Is the use of heroin increasing, peaking or decreasing?

This chapter presents the findings of our research into the numbers and characteristics of known drug users in Wirral during one year across 1984–5. It also links with Chapter 3, which reports on a second survey of known drug users conducted during the following year (1985–6), and in which, with the aid of a theoretical model of outbreaks of heroin use, we attempt to use our research findings to forecast future trends in heroin use.

In the remainder of this chapter, we will first briefly describe the methods of the survey of known drug users, and then turn to an examination of the findings.

Methods of investigation

Producing a reasonably accurate estimate of the overall number (prevalence) of illicit drug users in a community is a difficult task, not least because many people will not admit to illegal activities for fear of prosecution. Furthermore, conducting a random sample survey of even 5 per cent of Wirral's 260,000 adult residents would have been both very expensive and extremely time-consuming. Therefore, given the limitations on our time, resources and methods of investigation, we decided to adopt a two-pronged approach to estimating the prevalence of heroin use, a strategy developed by the London-based Drug Indicators Project (Hartnoll *et al.* 1985a). This involved a survey of the records of official agencies concerning known drug users (multi-agency enumeration); and interviews with natural networks of heroin users to establish the ratio of the number of 'unknown' users to those known to official agencies (see Chapter 5).

Multi-agency enumeration

Enumerating known drug users involves contacting the management representatives of statutory and voluntary agencies whose clienteles include drug users, in order to obtain permission to collect information about these clients. In our case, this task was made easier by the presence of many of these top professionals on the Wirral Drug Abuse Committee, the sponsors of our research. However, four criteria of inclusion needed to be established before we started to 'count heads': the definition of a case, the geographical boundaries of the count, the time period, and the type of estimate.

Case
As stated earlier, rather than attempt such difficult tasks as counting all 'illegal drug users', 'regular drug users' or 'non-medical drug users', we decided to count all 'problem drug users'. Problem drug use was defined as any non-medical use of psychoactive drugs which leads to medical, social and/or legal problems, as evidenced by the involvement of official agencies (see Parker *et al.* 1986a, for details). Six categories of drug were focused upon:

opioids including heroin, methadone (Physeptone), dihydrocodeine (DF118), dipipanone (Diconal), and dextromoramide (Palfium);
barbiturates, including quinalbarbitone (Seconal), and amylobarbitone (Tuinal);
stimulants, including cocaine, amphetamines and other synthetic stimulants;
psychedelics, including LSD and 'magic mushrooms' (e.g. psilocybe)
inhalants (solvents and gases), including toluene (in glue), butane (in lighter fuel), and fluorocarbons (in aerosols); and
cannabis, including herb ('grass'), resin (hashish), and oil.

We decided to exclude users of legal drugs such as alcohol, tobacco and caffeine, and users of prescribed drugs, such as tranquillisers and other hypnosedatives (unless used in combination with one or more of the six study drugs), because these most prevalent forms of 'licit' drug use were outside the scope of our investigation.

After consultation with all relevant professional groups, ten agencies were selected as 'indicators' of problem drug use: four medical agencies (GPs, a hospital Psychiatric Unit, the regional Drug Dependency Unit (DDU), and the local Detoxification Unit); and six socio-legal agencies (the police, the probation service, social services, the Education Department, the Drugs Council, and the Home Office (Notified Addicts Index)).

Time

Cases were counted if they were known to the indicator agencies in the one-year period from 1 July 1984 to 30 June 1985. Thus, our survey was 'retrospective' because the research was carried out between July and October 1985.

Place

Not all cases known to the indicator agencies were examined, but only those who were resident in the Borough of Wirral during the specified time period. Homeless people known to Wirral agencies were also included.

Type of estimate

Our aim was to establish the total number of individual problem drug users in Wirral, a figure called 'prevalence'. However, adding up the cases known to each agency would produce an overestimate of prevalence because some problem drug users will be known to two or more agencies (for example, the police and probation service). We therefore needed to identify individuals in order to adjust the prevalence estimate for double or multiple counts. Since we were obliged to respect the confidentiality of agencies' records on clients, we did not collect names or addresses, but instead recorded the initials, date of birth and sex of each case. This provided a unique 'identity code' by which duplicate cases of the same individual could be detected, thus enabling a more accurate estimate of the prevalence of problem drug use. Finally, this numerical estimate was converted into a 'population rate', by calculating the number of known heroin users per 1,000 of the Wirral population. This allows more valid comparisons between population sub-groups (for example, age groups, occupational groups) and with other communities of different size.

Procedure

The basic information collected from all or most of the agencies included details of their drug-taking clients' age, sex, occupational status, area of residence and type of drugs used. Additional information about clients' social characteristics (for example, marital status) and drug-using behaviour (for example, method of use) was also collected from agencies which routinely recorded such details, namely GPs, the Drugs Council, and the Detoxification Unit.

There were two strategies for data collection. First, in the case of agencies which have no central recording systems containing details of their drug-using clients — GPs, social services, and the probation service — a postal questionnaire survey of all professionals operating in the Wirral branches of these services was conducted. Following several reminders, the final response rates were 91 per cent (29 out of 32) for probation officers, 58 per cent (49 out of 84) for social workers, and 46 per cent (81 out of 177) for GPs. Second, in the case of the other seven indicator agencies, which did have central recording systems, visits were made by members of the research team who transcribed all of the required information on to prestructured forms. All of the information was then coded and entered into a mainframe computer (IBM 3083), and analysed using the SPSSX statistical package.

Findings

Problem drug users

Our survey revealed a grand total of 2,193 cases of problem drug use known to the ten indicator agencies (see Table 2.1). Following the elimination of double or multiple counts of the same individual, a final count of 1,604 individuals was obtained. Adjustments to incorporate various factors which may have affected this annual prevalence figure (over 200 cases lacking an identity code, low response rates from GPs and social workers) suggest a possible range of 1,550 to 1,850 individual problem drug users in Wirral during 1984–5.

Since many of these problem drug users were known to have taken or be taking more than one drug, they were classified according to a hierarchy of six drug-use categories, in order to simplify the numerous kinds of polydrug use

Table 2.1 Problem drug users known to official agencies during 1984–5

| | Problem drug users | | | | Known opioid users | | | |
| | All cases | | Unique Individuals | | All cases | | Unique Individuals | |
	N	(%)*	N	(%)	N	(%)*	N	(%)
Home Office	273	(17)	123	(8)	273	(21)	123	(9)
GPs	217	(14)	124	(8)	205	(16)	113	(9)
Psychiatric Unit	4	(<1)	3	(<1)	3	(<1)	2	(<1)
Detoxification Unit	315	(20)	124	(8)	313	(24)	123	(9)
Regional DDU	51	(3)	31	(2)	49	(4)	30	(2)
Social Services	63	(4)	47	(3)	35	(3)	21	(2)
Probation Service	407	(25)	222	(14)	353	(27)	179	(14)
Drugs Council	235	(15)	111	(7)	224	(17)	105	(8)
Education Department	28	(2)	16	(1)	3	(<1)	2	(<1)
Police	600	(37)	391	(24)	390	(30)	211	(16)
Individuals known to two or more agencies	NA		412	(26)	NA		396	(30)
Total	2,193		1,604	(100)	1,848		1,305	(100)

*Percentage of total number of unique individuals known to each agency.

exhibited. The drug categories were ranked according to an assessment of their 'problem-causing' potential, particularly as regards such problems as addiction, overdose, disease, and temporary deficits in skills needed to operate machinery (for example, to drive a car). Of course, any classification of drug users will be somewhat arbitrary and open to debate, and the present scheme was devised for practical reasons rather than as a conceptual model. Opioid use is the top category, and individuals in this group may also have been using any of the drugs in the other five categories. Barbiturates are the second hierarchical category, and individuals in this group may have been using any of the drugs in the four categories below, but not opioids. The categories continue to operate in this hierarchical fashion until we reach the sixth and final class: cannabis. Users in this group were not known to be taking any drug other than cannabis (though, like any drug user, they may have taken other drugs without official knowledge of this).

Four out of every five problem drug users were found to be opioid users, the only other salient group being cannabis users, the majority of whom were known only through police arrests for possession (see Table 2.2). Since British research in the 1980s has consistently found that the use of cannabis, amphetamines, psychedelics and inhalants is much more prevalent than the use of opioids (see Chapter 8), the present findings imply that users of the former drugs are far less likely than opioid users to develop 'officially recognised' problems (with the exception of legal problems, for example being prosecuted for possessing drugs). The remainder of this chapter therefore focuses on the main group of problem drug users: those who use opioids (see Parker *et al.* 1986a, for a description of all known drug users).

Table 2.2   Drug users in six hierarchical categories

Users of	Number	(%)
Opioids	1,305	(81)
Barbiturates	7	(<1)
Stimulants	31	(2)
Psychedelics	11	(1)
Inhalants	38	(2)
Cannabis	204	(13)
Not identified	8	(<1)
Total	1,604	(100)

Known opioid users

Drugs used
Table 2.1 shows that 1,305 of the 1,848 cases of opioid use known to official agencies were individual users of heroin or related drugs. Twenty people were found to have been primarily using opioids other than heroin (either

methadone or dihydrocodeine). Forty-one per cent of the known opioid users were also known to have taken other types of drug, although this is probably an underestimate since some agencies do not routinely record or receive information about all drugs used by people on their files. Cannabis was the most popular secondary drug, having been used by 38 per cent of known opioid users, followed by psychedelics (15 per cent) and stimulants (14 per cent).

The rate of known opioid use
The overall rate of known opioid use in the adult population of Wirral was found to be almost 5 per 1,000, but rates were clearly higher for males (over 6 per 1,000), 16–24-year-olds (over 18 per 1,000), and for the unemployed (about 28 per 1,000) (see Table 2.3, p.22).

Sex and age
There were 3.6 male heroin users for every female, with most agencies reporting a ratio close to this, the exceptions being the police and the probation service (5:1 at each). The dates of birth of 90 per cent of the known opioid users were obtained, and their average (modal) age at the mid-point of the prevalence period was 19 years. Two salient age groups can be distinguished: the 16–30 age group, which contains all ages comprising at least 1 per cent of the users (92 per cent of all users); and the 18–22 age group, which contains the five ages which each comprised at least 5 per cent of the users (56 per cent of all users). Only 14 users (1 per cent) were aged under 16 years, and there were no unexpected age differences between male and female opioid users or those known to different agencies. In short, the vast majority of known opioid users were adults younger than 30 years, and over half were aged 18–22 years.

Occupational status
Details of the occupational status of 903 (69 per cent) of the known opioid users were available, and it was found that 734 (81 per cent) were unemployed. This is an unemployment rate of 87 per cent among those users available for work, compared to 21 per cent in the general population of Wirral in June 1985 (24 per cent for males, and 15 per cent for females). The only other occupational group comprising more than 2 per cent were those in manual employment (9 per cent).

Other social characteristics
The marital status of most of the opioid users known to two drugs agencies were obtained: the Drugs Council, which attracted users seeking therapy and counselling, and the Detoxification Unit, which attracted users more likely to be seeking medical treatment. It was found that 78 per cent of 219 users at the Drugs Council and 72 per cent of 197 users at the Detoxification Unit were single (i.e. neither married nor cohabiting). Married or cohabiting users accounted for 16 per cent of those known to the Drugs Council, and 22 per cent of those known to the Detoxification Unit. Only 27 per cent (153) of the Drugs Council users and 31 per cent (61) of those at the Detoxification Unit lived in their own accommodation, and all but a few of the remaining majority

lived with parents or relatives (70 per cent at the Drugs Council, and 66 per cent at the Detoxification Unit). Nine out of ten of the users known to each agency lived with one or more adults, and the majority lived with one or more children. Single parents comprised about 4–5 per cent of the opioid users known to these agencies. In short, the typical opioid user known to both of these agencies was single and living with her or his family.

Information about the partners and families of clients of the Detoxification Unit was also obtained. Of 88 opioid users in stable relationships, 43 per cent stated that their partner also used drugs. Furthermore, 18 per cent of 185 opioid users stated that a member of their family also used drugs.

Finally, of 169 opioid users whose educational qualifications were known, 52 per cent had passed no examinations, 30 per cent had CSEs only, 17 per cent had passed O levels, and 1 per cent had A levels.

Details of heroin use
Three agencies — the Drugs Council, the Detoxification Unit, and GPs — were able to provide information about the frequency and duration of heroin use, the quantities used, and the route of administration (method of use).

Frequency   The vast majority of heroin users were daily users of the drug at the time of contact with these agencies: 208 out of 215 known to the Drugs Council, 166 out of 171 known to GPs, and all 242 known to the Detoxification Unit. However, this does not necessarily imply that virtually all use of heroin leads to a daily habit, but only that those who contact these agencies have established daily use of the drug.

Duration   The average duration of use of heroin by clients of the three agencies is about one to three years, a habit length which accounts for about half to two-thirds of the users known to each agency. Over 90 per cent of the heroin users at each agency had been using the drug for between one month and five years. Since the survey was based on clients known to agencies during 1984–5, these findings indicate that the initiators of this 'wave' of heroin use began using heroin in 1980–81. This is consistent both with Home Office figures for the annual number of notified drug addicts resident in Wirral during the 1980s (rising from four in 1980 to 320 in 1985), and with the experiences and estimates of local professionals concerned with heroin use. Finally, it was also found that the average self-reported first age of use of heroin by 236 clients of the Detoxification Unit was 17 years, with the age range 16–18 years accounting for nearly half of all reported first ages of heroin use.

Route   The commonest route of administration of heroin was by 'chasing the dragon', that is, heating the heroin and inhaling the smoke through a makeshift funnel. Smoking was the only known method of use of four in five of the clients of the three agencies. Injection was the sole route of use of less than 4 per cent of the clients, but in combination with other methods (smoking and sniffing), injection was used by one in ten of the users. Furthermore, a quarter of the combined cases of the Drugs Council and the Detoxification

Unit were known to have tried injecting heroin. The serious implications of these practices in relation to the spread of infection are discussed in Chapter 9, once we have noted (in Chapters 4 and 5) that agency records actually underestimate the amount of injecting taking place.

Quantity   The amount of heroin reported to be used by 195 daily users known to the Drugs Council and 207 daily users known to the Detoxification Unit varied between one £5 'bag' per day (enough for a few 'hits') and 4 grams per day (costing up to £240). Of course, the amounts reported are approximate, and the purity of the heroin is unknown. The typical quantity of heroin used by 53 per cent of these users is 0.25–0.5 gram per day, which cost between £20 and £35 at that time. However, Drugs Council clients had over twice the proportion of 'two bag' daily users (22 per cent against 9 per cent) compared to clients of the Detoxification Unit, whereas the latter agency had nearly three times the proportion of 1 gram per day users (14 per cent against 5 per cent). It appears that heavier users may be more likely to 'medicalise' their dependence and seek either prescribed drugs or detoxification, whereas lighter users may be more likely to view their drug-related problems as requiring a counselling service.

Social deprivation
Known opioid use in Wirral was found to be heavily concentrated in the larger, socially deprived communities. Information about the area of residence of 1,137 (87 per cent) of the known opioid users was obtained. Four of Wirral's 48 townships clearly have the highest rates of known opioid use, both in their overall and youth populations. Figure 2.1 illustrates the pattern for 16–24-year-olds, identifying Ford and Woodchurch as the most affected areas, followed by Birkenhead and Wallasey Village. The residents of these four townships constitute 12 per cent of Wirral's total population, yet between them they contain 38 per cent of the borough's known opioid users. Indeed, adjusting the figures to take account of those whose area of residence was not known, it can be calculated that one in ten youths on the most affected estate were known heroin users during 1984–5. This township also had the highest rate of unemployment in Wirral during this time (33 per cent), and its residents were enduring high levels of social deprivation.

    In order further to investigate this implied relationship between heroin use and social deprivation, we employed 1981 Census statistics to examine correlations between the rate of known opioid use and levels of social deprivation in each of Wirral's 48 townships (unemployment figures were for May 1985, and included temporarily sick residents). Significant positive correlations were found between the rate of known opioid use and each of seven indicators of social deprivation (in both the general and youth populations), namely: unemployment, council tenancies, overcrowding, large families, single-parent households, an unskilled labour force, and having no access to a car (see Parker *et al.* 1986a). There was also a relatively minor but significant correlation between the rate of known opioid use and townships' population size.

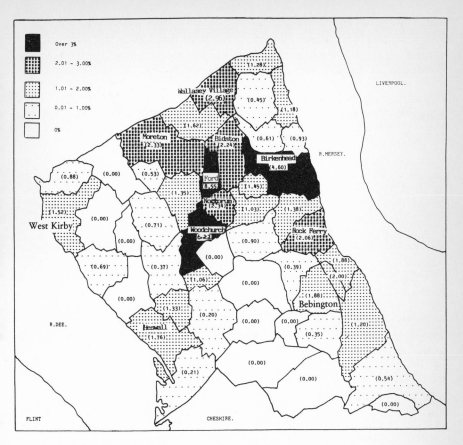

Figure 2.1   16–24-year-old heroin users by township (per cent)

Comparisons of the 48 townships, ranked according to rates of known opioid use, unemployment (the most highly correlated indicator of social deprivation), and population size, confirm the strength of the correlations and also spotlight salient exceptions. For instance, the ten townships with the highest rates of known opioid use (average 0.7 per cent) have a mean population size of about 10,000, and a mean unemployment rate of 20 per cent. By contrast, as might be expected, the nine townships with a zero rate of known opioid use have a much lower mean population size of about 1,300, and a much lower mean unemployment rate of 6 per cent.

However, there were four notable exceptions to these general correlations. First, there are two clear examples of townships with high rates of known opioid use but relatively low rates of unemployment: Wallasey Village (ranked fourth for opioid use but 33rd for unemployment), and Heswall (11th against 37th). Second, this deviation from the general trend was also exhibited to a lesser extent by Bebington (9th against 28th) and West Kirby (14th against

28th). There were no notable examples of townships with high unemployment but low rates of known opioid use.

One compelling interpretation of these exceptional deviations from the general correlation between opioid use and social deprivation derives from the epidemiological model of heroin use developed by researchers in the USA (for example, Hunt and Chambers 1976; Richman and Abbey 1977). Two complementary processes of 'diffusion' are proposed to explain how heroin use spreads through the population: microdiffusion and macrodiffusion. Microdiffusion is compatible with deviance theorists' emphasis on deviant lifestyles having to be learnt (see Becker 1963). It describes a social-psychological process whereby heroin and its associated cultural knowledge (for instance, how to use it) are spread by means of communication and exchange between individuals who live in close proximity to one another, but who may be from different social groups. Macrodiffusion is a higher-level process by which outbreaks of heroin use emerge in the most densely populated cities and towns, and gradually spread to less heavily populated areas. Evidence in support of this social process is provided by our finding of a significant correlation between the rates of known opioid use in Wirral townships and their population size.

The high rates of known opioid use in Wallasey Village and Bebington may be partly or wholly explained by microdiffusion processes. That is, although social deprivation in these townships is comparatively low, some of their neighbouring townships have high levels of social deprivation and known opioid use (such as Bidston, Birkenhead, Ford and Moreton in the former case, and Rock Ferry and New Ferry in the latter case). The sharing of pubs, clubs, cafés, schools, parks and street corners within a densely populated urban area encompassing several townships is probably the main vehicle of this inter-personal and inter-group transmission of the heroin habit.

The explanation of the high rates of known opioid use in West Kirby and Heswall needs to be somewhat different, since neither is very close to any township with high levels of known opioid use or social deprivation. These townships are two of the most 'well-heeled' communities in Wirral's most middle-class area, Deeside. However, they are also the largest towns in Deeside, and so, by a process of macrodiffusion, would be the first towns in the area to experience outbreaks of heroin use. Indeed, this model is consistent with the general pattern of known heroin use throughout Deeside. For instance, in the case of both West Kirby and Heswall, the only neighbouring townships with rates of known opioid use higher than 2 per 1,000 are the next most densely populated urban areas of Deeside (Hoylake and Pensby respectively), with eight of the other 14 smaller townships in Deeside having no known opioid users. Of course, middle-class users are also more likely to avoid contact with statutory and voluntary agencies for several reasons (such as private treatment, or fewer financial problems), an important consideration to which we will return in later chapters.

The diffusion model of the spread of heroin use in Wirral will be further examined in Chapter 3, which reports on a second multi-agency survey of known opioid users during 1985–6, and presents a forecast of the future of heroin use in Wirral.

Comparison with other areas

Having established that the annual prevalence of known opioid use in Wirral during 1984–5 was about 5 per 1,000 of the adult population, the question arises as to how high this level of opioid use is compared to other areas of the UK. This section first compares prevalence in Wirral with the few studies of rates of opioid use in other parts of the UK, and then turns to an examination of the characteristics of opioid users in different areas.

Prevalence

Official statistics about illegal drug use in the UK are pitifully inadequate. Central government has neither conducted a national survey of illegal drug use nor developed an adequate system of monitoring known cases other than those identified by medical practitioners — who are anyway partial and negligent in their notifying practices. This means that national statistics gathered by the Home Office, via its Notifications Index, greatly underestimate levels of opioid use, probably by a factor of between three and ten. However, although of little value in terms of estimating the prevalence of heroin use, the official statistics (notifications and convictions) do give some indication of regional differences in prevalence since figures are disaggregated by police force and health authority area.

Merseyside was consistently second or third in the official 'league tables' for illegal drug use in the United Kingdom during 1985 (after the Metropolitan Police District, which includes London, and sometimes after Strathclyde, which includes Glasgow). This high ranking holds for seizures of heroin, persons found guilty of drug offences, and new and former drug addicts notified to the Home Office (Home Office 1986).

However, there are two further difficulties with these official statistics as regards comparisons between different areas. First, they tell us only about absolute numbers of drug users or drug-related events, and not about population rates. Finding the largest numbers of drug users in our largest cities and towns does not necessarily imply that they have proportionately more drug users than smaller communities. Second, the geographical breakdown of the official statistics is by police force areas, which do not correspond to the areas for which Census population statistics are available, and which submerge figures for Wirral in the Merseyside figures.

Consequently, valid comparisons of the rate of known opioid use in Wirral with the rates in other areas of the UK depend upon an assessment of the findings of the handful of local surveys of known drug users in the 1980s. Of the five multi-agency enumeration surveys conducted by the time the Wirral research was completed, two were in northern communities (Greater Glasgow and South Tyneside) and three in southern communities (within Avon, Lon-

don and Sussex). Since all five surveys differ with respect to their methods of
investigation and the type of estimate made, the figures used to indicate the
rate of known opioid use in Wirral have been adjusted to increase the validity
of each comparison (see Table 2.3).

The first research team to investigate the prevalence of opioid use through
multi-agency surveys and fieldwork was the London-based Drug Indicators
Project (Hartnoll *et al.* 1985b). This study produced three age-related
estimates of 'regular opioid use' in the London boroughs of Camden and
Islington (based on research from 1977 to 1983): 12 per 1,000 of the
16–24-year-old population, 25 per 1,000 of the 25–34-year-olds, and 5 per
1,000 of the 35–44-year-olds. Although the differences between 'regular' and
'problematic' opioid users, and between all users and known users, rule out a
straightforward comparison of the levels of opioid use in the two areas, it is
apparent that Wirral opioid users were more concentrated in the 16–24-year-
old population (18 per 1,000), and relatively less concentrated in the two older
age groups (about 6 per 1,000 25–34-year-olds and 0.5 per 1,000 35–44-year-
olds).

Table 2.3   Wirral's annual rates of problem drug use and known opioid use,
1984–5

Population	Size	Problem drug users		Known opioid users	
		Number	Rate*	Number	Rate*
Overall	338,952	1,604	4.7	1,305	3.9
Adults	262,149	1,526	5.8	1,291	4.9
Males	162,186	1,264	7.8	1,010	6.2
Females	176,766	328	1.9	283	1.6
5–15	56,335	78	1.4	14	0.2
16–24	47,706	1,026	21.5	870	18.2
25–34	45,660	289	6.3	250	5.5
35–44	38,942	35	0.9	21	0.5
45 +	150,444	13	0.1	5	<0.1
Unemployed	26,478	826	31.2	734	27.7
Males	19,082	672	35.2	583	30.6
Females	7,396	154	20.8	146	19.7

*Per 1,000 population.

N.B. The number/rates by sex, age-group and unemployment are underestimates because the sex,
age and/or occupational status of some individuals were unknown, and so these individuals are
not included in the breakdown. Population figures are based on 1981 Census statistics; unemployment figures are for May 1985.

Second, a study of problem drug users known to eight agencies in the South
Tyneside area during a six-month period in 1981 (Pattison *et al.* 1982) produced an estimated annual prevalence rate of 1.2 known opioid users per
1,000 of the adult population, compared to about 5 per 1,000 in Wirral.

However, given the overall rise in heroin use in Britain during the 1980s, it seems plausible that the rate of known opioid use would have increased in South Tyneside between 1981 and the middle of the decade. Nevertheless, research which examined heroin use in several communities across the North of England in 1985 (Pearson *et al.* 1986) concluded that Tyneside and other communities in the North-East continued to have a relatively low prevalence of heroin use compared with cities and towns in the North-West.

Third, a study in Greater Glasgow (Haw 1985) investigated problem drug use during the years 1980–83 using routine statistics, and by a prospective survey of four agencies and fieldwork in two areas of Glasgow during the first three months of 1984. The annual prevalence rate for the entire population of Greater Glasgow in 1983 was estimated at about 4 known opioid users per 1,000 — the same as in Wirral. However, since the Glasgow study began 18 months earlier than the Wirral survey, and since prevalence was estimated to be on the increase, it is possible that the rate of known opioid use in Glasgow exceeded that in Wirral by 1984–5.

Fourth, a study in the Brighton Health Authority area (Levy 1985) investigated problem drug users known to a dozen agencies during 1984, producing an estimated annual prevalence rate of 1.5 known opioid users per 1,000 of the 15–35-year-old population. The closest comparable figure for Wirral is the annual prevalence rate for the 16–34-year-old age group: 12 per 1,000. Even allowing for differences between the two surveys, it seems fairly likely that the rate of known opioid use was much higher in Wirral than Brighton during 1984 and 1985.

Fifth, an interim report of the Avon Drug Abuse Monitoring Project (Gay *et al.* 1985), which investigated problem drug users known to a dozen agencies during the one-year period ending March 1985, reported an estimated annual prevalence rate of 0.5 known opioid users per 1,000 of the total Bristol population. The methods employed in this study were very similar to those adopted in the Wirral survey, which had a comparable annual prevalence rate of 4 per 1,000, clearly a much higher rate of known opioid use than in Bristol during this period.

In summary, a review of research on levels of opioid use in the 1980s suggests that Wirral, along with London and Glasgow, had one of the highest recorded rates of known opioid use in the UK at the mid-point of the decade. However, it should be emphasised that the above comparisons gloss over several differences between the studies, and will become quickly outdated as heroin outbreaks emerge in other areas during the second half of the decade and the 1990s.

Characteristics

The findings of our survey can be summarised to produce the following picture of the typical 'officially known' Wirral heroin user: a young, unemployed, single person (usually male), living with his or her family in a socially deprived area, with few or no educational qualifications. The typical known user had been smoking heroin daily for about one to three years, having started the habit around the age of 16–18, and was using 0.25–0.5 gram of heroin per day (costing between £20 and £35) at the time of agency contact.

This profile of the 'new wave' heroin user is clearly different from that characterising the 'first wave' of heroin users in the late 1960s and early 1970s. In contrast to the young family-based heroin smokers of Wirral in the 1980s, the earlier London-based users were largely in the 25–35 age range, of more 'bohemian' lifestyle, and preferred injection as their primary method of taking heroin (see Stimson and Oppenheimer 1982; and Jameson et al. 1984). Many, if not most, were also part of the 'hippie' subculture, whereas the new heroin users in Wirral were largely 'ordinary' youths with no obvious strong allegiances to contemporary subcultures such as 'punk' (see Chapters 4 and 5).

There were also several differences between the profile of known Wirral heroin users and the 'new' heroin users described by the surveys in other parts of the UK during the 1980s. First, the majority of Wirral users appeared to be much younger. For instance, of the estimated 2,100 regular opioid users in Camden and Islington in 1983, about 70 per cent were aged 25 years or older, and only 5 per cent were aged between 16 and 19 years. Similarly, in the survey of 174 problem drug users in Brighton (90 per cent of whom were opioid users), 57 per cent were aged 26 years or older, and just 17 per cent were aged between 15 and 20 years. Indeed, the average age of new narcotic addicts notified to the Home Office in 1984 was about 26 years. Yet, the modal age of the known Wirral user was 19 years: only 17 per cent were aged 26 years or older, and almost 40 per cent were aged 20 years or younger. However, the Glasgow profile, with a peak age range of 20–24 years, does come much closer to the Wirral peak range of 18–22 years.

Furthermore, it has been reported that the majority of heroin users in Glasgow, Edinburgh and London preferred to inject heroin, as did up to 400 users in a study in Leeds in 1985 (Polley et al. 1986), whereas smoking heroin was, at the time of the first survey, the preferred route of administration for four out of five known Wirral users. The spread of HIV infection through the medium of shared injection equipment would therefore appear to be less likely among Wirral users compared to other major cities in the UK where heroin users mostly inject their drugs. The validity of this statement, however, depends on whether agencies obtain accurate information about injecting, particularly casual/occasional injecting, and whether increasingly long-term users are willing to stick with 'chasing'. We will provide some evidence, from our ethnographic work, to show that the complete picture is much more complex, and highly fluid.

Turning to the sex of known opioid users, the 3.6:1 male to female ratio found for Wirral opioid users is somewhat higher than the 2.7:1 ratio found for problem drug users (mostly heroin users) in both Brighton and South Tyneside, and the 2:1 ratio reported for opioid users in both Bristol and Leeds. The lower proportion of females among known users in Wirral was particularly evident in relation to Camden and Islington, where the male–female ratio was 1.8:1. Furthermore, the Wirral ratio is also higher than the 2.4:1 ratio characterising new narcotic addicts notified to the Home Office in 1984. As in the case of age characteristics, Glasgow may be most similar to Wirral with respect to the sex ratio of known opioid users (see Haw 1985).

Although the unemployment rate in Wirral in 1985 stood at 20 per cent, 87 per cent of the borough's known opioid users were unemployed, and strong correlations were found throughout the borough between level of opioid use, unemployment and social deprivation. The Brighton study also investigated the occupational status of 154 problem drug users (90 per cent opioid users), and found that 72 per cent of those available for work were unemployed, compared to 16 per cent in the total 17–35-year-old population. Furthermore, a three-phase study of over a thousand school leavers in the Lothian region of Scotland found that, in marked contrast to alcohol and tobacco use, 'levels of illicit drug use were much higher amongst both males and females who were unemployed than amongst their peers who were working or were full-time students' (Plant *et al.* 1985, p. 6). A more detailed analysis of the data revealed a significant association between the duration of unemployment and use of illegal drugs such as heroin (Peck and Plant 1986). This article also carefully considers several other sources of evidence linking unemployment, urban deprivation and heroin use, and argues that 'the most parsimonious conclusion is that high unemployment serves to foster drug use' (ibid., p. 931).

It therefore appears that, although the Wirral heroin users differed from users in other parts of the UK in being younger, more predominantly male, and typically smokers of heroin, they shared with 'new' users throughout the country the characteristics of unemployment and relative poverty. Therefore, assuming that the supply of heroin remains strong, it is reasonable to predict that future levels of heroin use will continue to mirror any increases in unemployment or poverty, though a decline in social deprivation will not necessarily be accompanied by a drop in the prevalence of heroin use. This is because regular heroin use is likely to result in both physical addiction and a major psychological dependence, and these consequences would keep prevalence at a high level long after any drop in the level of social deprivation.

However, more detailed scientific forecasts of trends in heroin use depend upon both a theoretical model of the spread of heroin use, and data from two or more points in time to examine projected trends in heroin use. The next chapter explains how this conceptual framework allowed us to construct a forecast of the course of the Wirral heroin 'epidemic'.

3

Here today, here tomorrow: monitoring and forecasting trends in heroin use

Our survey of official agencies in contact with drug users revealed over 1,300 Wirral residents known to use opioids in 1984–5, about 5 per 1,000 of the adult population. However, in order to make recommendations to the borough about how to plan services for the future, we also needed to forecast trends in heroin use. This meant providing informed answers to a number of questions. Will the prevalence of heroin use increase, decline or become stable? Would heroin users turn from smoking to injecting? Would there be a noticeable diffusion of heroin use from the areas of urban social deprivation to more middle-class communities and smaller towns? Given the complex, multi-causal nature of the use of heroin and other drugs, constructing accurate projections of drug-taking behaviour is extremely difficult, and ideally requires large, longitudinal studies. However, we approached this task by conducting a second multi-agency enumeration survey of problem drug users during 1985–6. It was hoped that the combined findings of our two annual surveys, in conjunction with a theoretical model of heroin 'epidemics', would provide some modest foundations for making tentative hypotheses about future trends. The first part of this chapter describes the conceptual framework underlying our predictions about heroin use in Wirral, and is followed by an account of our second survey of problem drug use and our forecasts of future prevalence. The final section discusses some of the conceptual and methodological problems associated with these projections. Finally, it should be noted that the forecasts of future prevalence discussed in this chapter pertain only to changes in the size of the known user population. The 'true community prevalence' of opioid use (i.e. the total number of known and unknown opioid users) is estimated and discussed in Chapter 5.

A model of the heroin 'epidemic'

Our forecast of the future of heroin use in Wirral has its foundations in epidemiology, the scientific study of epidemics. Strictly speaking, 'epidemic' refers to an increase in new cases of a contagious disease from a previously stable, 'endemic' level of new cases (see, for example, Barker and Rose 1979). However, we borrowed this term to describe the outbreak of heroin use in Wirral during the 1980s because of the epidemic-like characteristics of this phenomenon, such as its transmission through individual contact and the rapid increase in new users during the early part of the decade. Our use of this metaphor is not intended to imply that heroin use is a physical disease with viral or organic origins. As will become clearer in the following chapters, we believe it is more constructive to view the use of heroin or other drugs as a complex social behaviour determined by a multiplicity of causes, not least of which is the normal human desire to 'feel high' (be happy) in an increasingly hedonistic world. Nevertheless, we adopt the 'epidemic' metaphor in this chapter not just as convenient shorthand for an increase in heroin use, but rather because of its pivotal role in a theoretical framework which allows projections of future trends to be constructed. Of course, a more sophisticated model of trends in drug use would also incorporate the effects of economic forces, political factors and cultural variables, but such an all-embracing, comprehensive theory was beyond the scope of our time-limited, local research project. A brief description of our forecasting model follows.

Some basic concepts needed to describe the prevalence of heroin use were introduced in Chapter 2, namely: case (whom to count), time (when to count), and place (where to count). We also briefly discussed macrodiffusion and microdiffusion, concepts which describe the geographical and demographic spread of heroin 'epidemics'. But in order to understand changes in the number of heroin users across time we need to unpack and examine the two opposing components of prevalence: incidence and outcidence.[1]

As illustrated in Figure 3.1, the total number of heroin users in a community during a one-year period (annual prevalence) is analogous to the level of water in a sink. This level is influenced by two other factors: the number of new heroin users who emerge during this period (annual incidence), and the number of users who cease to take heroin during this period (annual outcidence). The incidence figure is primarily made up of novice users, but also includes some recidivists (for example, former users who have decided to take heroin again). Outcidence is the opposite of incidence, and primarily consists of those users who stop taking heroin, but also includes a small proportion of users who die or move away from the area of study. Incidence is analogous to water pouring into a sink and outcidence is analogous to water leaving the sink via the plughole.

This metaphor allows us to see more clearly how changes in annual prevalence are related to the opposing forces of incidence and outcidence. There are three general scenarios. If annual incidence is equal to annual outcidence (water is pouring into the sink at the same rate as it is emptying), then annual prevalence remains at a stable, unchanging level (the water level in

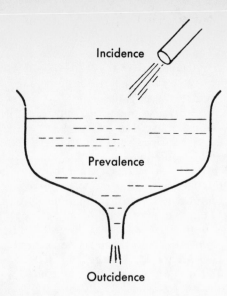

Incidence

Prevalence

Outcidence

Figure 3.1   Sink model of prevalence

the sink is constant). But, if annual incidence exceeds outcidence (water enters the sink at a faster rate than it exits), then annual prevalence increases (the water level in the sink rises). Finally, if incidence falls below outcidence (water is pouring into the sink at a slower rate than it is draining off), there will be a decrease in annual prevalence (the water level in the sink drops).

So, an 'epidemic' of heroin use occurs when incidence rises (above the normal, endemic level of use) and continues to rise at a rate higher than the outcidence rate. However, incidence 'peaks' when heroin use has 'saturated' most of the population likely to try the drug, and then begins to fall as it approaches saturation point. Nevertheless, if incidence starts to fall while outcidence remains stable, prevalence continues to rise, albeit at a decreasing rate, and begins to fall only when incidence drops below the level of outcidence. Of course, one cornerstone of this model of the structure of heroin 'epidemics' is the questionable assumption that only a certain proportion of the population are likely to take heroin, the corollary assumption being that the 'epidemic' must have a life cycle because it will eventually exhaust the pool of potential heroin users. Graphically represented, this means that heroin 'epidemics' will be negatively skewed (see Figure 3.2).

Drawing on American research on heroin 'epidemics', we can also add empirical 'meat' to this conceptual framework. Hunt and Chambers (1976) conclude from their epidemiological research that heroin use becomes 'epidemic' when a group of 'susceptibles' is exposed to many 'infectious initiators' at the same time. They argue that the time period in which the heroin 'epidemic' runs its course has a fixed length, due to the speed at which this 'infectious behaviour' saturates the 'susceptible' population by the

Level of
heroin
use

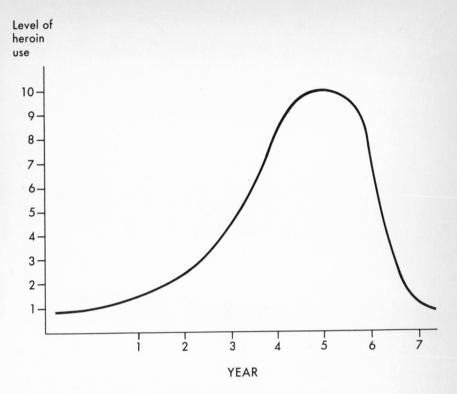

Figure 3.2   A schematic model of a heroin 'epidemic'

processes of microdiffusion and macrodiffusion. Briefly, their 'epidemic'
model proposes that, from a stable endemic baseline, the number of new cases
of heroin use (incidence) in a community increases rapidly for four years before
peaking at ten times the level of initial endemic incidence in year five, and then
dropping sharply to the previous endemic level during years six and seven (see
Figure 3.2). There have also been suggestions that local heroin 'epidemics'
recur at intervals of 15–20 years, though why this should be so is not clear.

We will turn a more critical eye to the assumptions and propositions of this
model in the final part of this chapter. The next section reports on our second
multi-agency enumeration survey, which provided the empirical component of
our forecast of Wirral's heroin 'epidemic'.

A second survey of problem drug use, 1985–6

In addition to our aim of forecasting the course of Wirral's heroin 'epidemic',
the second multi-agency enumeration survey also allowed us to investigate
whether there had been any changes in the social and drug-using

characteristics of known heroin users over the two years of research. In particular, we were interested in examining whether there were any changes in the age distribution of known heroin users, whether heroin use had spread from the most socially deprived areas to adjacent areas and middle-class communities, and whether there were any indications that heroin users were turning from 'chasing the dragon' (smoking) to injecting heroin.

Clearly, the issue of injecting, important as it was prior to the arrival of HIV infection, because of the risks of hepatitis and other disorders, is now of paramount importance to the whole international community. The spread of HIV infection has become the major public health issue of the century. Moreover, research on the transmission of the virus in the USA suggests that it is drug injectors who are 'the main source for any future heterosexual epidemic' (Moss 1987, p.389). Consequently, those British cities and towns which have large numbers of people using injectable drugs may be among the first to experience full-blown AIDS/HIV epidemics, not just because needle-sharing can spread the virus between drug users, but because infected drug users — particularly the young and single — are likely to spread the virus to the wider population through sexual contacts. The tendency of some heroin users, particularly females, to finance their habit through prostitution, further enhances the likelihood of HIV spreading to the wider community through this transmission route. The Scottish experience, most notably in Edinburgh, where the majority of drug injectors are believed to be infected by the virus (Robertson *et al*. 1986), has sounded the shrillest of warnings. Wirral, at the time of writing, is in the enviable position of having the opportunity to respond to any switch from smoking to injecting heroin, and of ensuring that those drug users who do inject have clean equipment and are aware of the risks (cf. Newcombe 1987b).

Methods of investigation

The procedures employed to conduct the second multi-agency enumeration survey were similar to those adopted in the first survey, the main differences being the need to revise the agencies employed to enumerate problem drug users (see Parker *et al*. 1986a, 1987a, for a detailed account of the methodology). In brief, we counted each Wirral resident known by our indicator agencies to have used, in the one-year period July 1985 to June 1986, one or more drugs in the following six categories: opioids, barbiturates, stimulants, psychedelics, inhalants, or cannabis. A final total of unique individuals was obtained by employing the 'duplicate elimination' procedure described in Chapter 2.

The second prevalence survey employed eight indicator agencies: six of the ten agencies used in the first survey (Home Office, police, probation service, Detoxification Unit, Drugs Council, and Education Department) and two additional agencies, the Wirral Committee on Solvent Abuse, and the Society for Biophysical Medicine. The latter Liverpool-based agency, which offers electro-acupuncture treatment to drug-dependent people, opened in December 1985, and soon began to attract clients from the Wirral area.

Four agencies employed in the first survey were excluded for various reasons. First, Social Services and GPs were not approached because of their low response rates in the first survey. Second, the Regional Alcohol and Drug Dependency Unit and the Psychiatric Ward of a local hospital were excluded largely because of the small and decreasing numbers of Wirral drug users approaching these agencies since the opening of the Detoxification Unit at Wirral's main hospital. It is believed that substantial numbers of 'additional' known drug users may have been 'missed' only in the case of GPs (to whom 124 problem drug users were known exclusively in the first survey). However, given that our interviews with users have uncovered an increasing disillusionment of heroin users with GPs, and vice versa, and given the overlap between users known to GPs and the Home Office, it is possible that, even in the case of GPs, the number of problem drug users 'missed' is not that large.

The basic information collected and the procedures used to collect it were similar to those in the first survey (see Chapter 2). In the case of the Society for Biophysical Medicine, agency staff conducted the transcribing task themselves, and posted the information to the research project. Finally, probation officers were again surveyed by postal questionnaire, and, following a number of reminders, the final response rate was 40 per cent (19 out of 47). This is less than half the response rate obtained in the first survey (91 per cent).

Findings

Prevalence and incidence

Problem drug users   The second prevalence survey revealed a grand total of 1,372 cases of problem drug use known to the eight indicator agencies, which, after duplicates were eliminated, came down to 1,076 unique individual problem drug users (see Table 3.1). In order to produce an estimate of relative incidence (the number of known new cases), the identity codes of these drug users were then cross-referenced with those on the list of problem drug users for 1984–5. It was found that 599 (56 per cent) were classifiable as 'new cases', that is, as not being known to any of the agencies in the first survey, and having no known first contact date with an agency prior to April 1985. Thus, our two multi-agency enumeration surveys had identified more than 2,200 individual problem drug users in Wirral in the 24 months ending July 1986, which is a two-year prevalence rate of 8.4 per 1,000 of the adult population.

As in the 1984–5 survey, the vast majority of problem drug users (73 per cent) were opioid users. The only other common type of drug user was cannabis users (16 per cent), the vast majority of whom were known only to the police for possession of cannabis (see Table 3.2). It is therefore feasible to make projections of future trends only in the case of opioid use, and so the remainder of this section focuses on users of opioids, of whom 98.5 per cent (776 out of 788) primarily used heroin.

Known opioid users   There was a grand total of 1,045 cases of opioid use

Table 3.1   Problem drug users known to official agencies during 1985–6

Agency	Problem drug users				Known opioid users					
	All Cases		All Individuals		All Cases		All Individuals		New Individuals	
	N	(%)*	N	(%)	N	(%)*	N	(%)	N	(%)
Home Office Detoxification	172	(16)	91	(8)	172	(22)	91	(12)	69	(19)
Unit	231	(21)	123	(11)	218	(28)	113	(14)	41	(12)
Probation Service	280	(26)	206	(19)	248	(31)	182	(23)	55	(15)
Drugs Council	231	(21)	153	(14)	201	(26)	129	(16)	49	(14)
Education Department	41	(4)	36	(3)	–†		–†		–†	
Police	303	(28)	231	(21)	120	(15)	74	(9)	55	(15)
Solvents Committee	28	(3)	24	(2)	–		–		–	
Society for Biophysical Medicine	86	(8)	28	(3)	86	(11)	28	(4)	28	(8)
Individuals known to 2 + agencies		NA	184	(17)		NA	171	(22)	59	(17)
Total	1,372		1,076	(100)	1,045		788	(100)	356	(100)

*Percentage of all individuals known to agency
†The Education Department failed to provide details of the drugs used by children reported to them by schools

known to the eight indicator agencies during the year 1985–6, with 'duplicate elimination' resulting in a final count of 788 individuals. Almost four in five of these individuals were known exclusively to a single agency, with almost a quarter of all opioid users being known exclusively to the probation service.

The identity codes of these 788 opioid users were then cross-referenced with those on the list of known opioid users for 1984–5, giving a relative incidence count of 356 (that is to say, 45 per cent of all known opioid users were new cases). This means that, over a two-year period, we had identified 1,661 heroin users known to official agencies in Wirral — 6.3 per 1,000 of the adult population.

A crude comparison of the figure of 788 known opioid users in 1985–6 with the figure of 1,305 known opioid users in 1984–5 suggests a decrease in the prevalence of known opioid use. However, such a comparison is invalid for several reasons, some of which will be addressed in the concluding section of this chapter. We will now consider two slightly more sophisticated types of statistical comparison: an examination of the 'incidence–outcidence' relationship, and a more valid comparison of the two surveys using the adjusted figures for those agencies which were involved in both surveys.

Table 3.2 Drug users in six hierarchical categories

Users of	N	(%)
Opioids	788	(73)
Barbiturates	4	(<1)
Stimulants	25	(2)
Psychedelics	4	(<1)
Inhalants	44	(4)
Cannabis	174	(16)
Not identified	37	(3)
Total	1,076	(100)

First, our working model of the heroin 'epidemic' maintains that prevalence (all cases) will increase if incidence (new cases) outstrips outcidence (the number of individuals 'coming off' heroin), and conversely that prevalence will decrease if the outcidence rate exceeds the incidence rate. In addition, we assume an optimistic outcidence rate of 20 per cent, that is, that one in five opioid users in 1984–5 will not be opioid users during 1985–6 (this is based on the reported 'coming off' rate among clients of the Detoxification Unit during this period). This simple epidemiological model allows us to calculate that of the 1,305 cases of known opioid use in 1984–5, 261 will have stopped using opioids during the following year. Thus, since relative incidence (new cases of known opioid use) reached 356 during 1985–6, this suggests that prevalence had increased by a further 95 individuals. In short, even assuming the highest feasible outcidence rate, the number of heroin users in Wirral appeared to be still increasing.

However, for prevalence to have reached 1,305 by 1984–5, starting from a very low endemic baseline in 1979 (and assuming an acceleration in the incidence rate around 1982–3), annual incidence would have to have been higher than 400 or 500 during 1984 and 1985. If this was the case, then although the present analysis has concluded that the prevalence of known opioid use was still increasing in 1985–6, it also suggests that annual incidence had peaked and was declining. This model of the heroin 'epidemic' is depicted in Figure 3.3, and implies that the prevalence of known heroin use would peak around 1988–9. It also allows us to forecast that prevalence will also subsequently begin to decline. More sophisticated and complex computer models of the heroin 'epidemic' can be constructed to produce precise estimates for the future, but given the many untestable assumptions of 'epidemic' models (particularly those based only on figures for known users during a relatively short time period, as in the present case), we did not attempt such an exercise.

Furthermore, the above analysis may be justifiably criticised on the grounds that it compares two surveys which employed different agencies to reach their estimates of the prevalence of known opioid use. Consequently, an alternative projection of future trends was attempted by comparing the figures obtained from those agencies who were involved in both surveys. Five agencies were

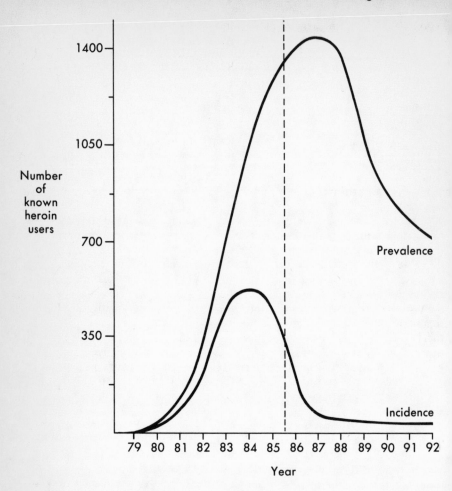

Figure 3.3 Model of the Wirral heroin 'epidemic'

continuously monitored across the two years in which the two surveys were conducted: the Home Office, the police, the probation service, the Detoxification Unit, and the Drugs Council. Seven hundred and sixty individual opioid users were known to these five agencies in 1985–6, compared with 1,135 in 1984–5 (see Table 3.3). On the basis of a crude comparison it appears that the prevalence of known opioid use has decreased by up to 400 cases. As described earlier, our model of the heroin 'epidemic' states that the relationship between incidence and outcidence determines prevalence, and assumes that annual outcidence is 20 per cent at the highest. Therefore, it can be calculated that of the 1,135 opioid users known to our five main indicator agencies in 1984–5, 227 would have 'come off' opioids by the following year. Thus, since relative incidence (new cases of known opioid use)

Table 3.3 Comparison of numbers of individual opioid users known to five
agencies monitored in 1984–5 and 1985–6

	All known opioid users		New known opioid users
	1984–5	1985–6	1985–6
	N (%)	N (%)	N (%)
Home Office	123 (11)	91 (12)	69 (21)
Detoxification Unit	123 (11)	113 (15)	41 (13)
Probation	179 (16)	182 (24)	55 (17)
Drugs Council	105 (9)	129 (17)	49 (15)
Police	211 (19)	74 (10)	55 (17)
Known to two or more agencies	394 (35)	171 (23)	59 (18)
Total	1,135 (100)	760 (100)	328 (100)

across the five agencies reached 328 during 1985–6, this suggests that
prevalence had increased by about a further 100 individuals. As argued earlier,
for prevalence to have risen to over 1,000 in 1984–5 from a very low baseline
in 1979 and a major acceleration in the incidence rate around 1982–3, annual
incidence for the five agencies must have been over 400 during 1984–5,
compared with nearer 300 in 1985–6. This is consistent with the hypothesis
that incidence had peaked and was probably declining — in other words, that
the present potential user population was beginning to approach 'saturation
point'. Thus, we could forecast that the prevalence curve was rising less steeply
and would peak around 1988–9. The likelihood of this future scenario is
further discussed in the final section of this chapter.

Social and drug-using characteristics
The social and drug-using characteristics of known opioid users in the second
prevalence survey were, by and large, similar to those found in the first survey
during 1984–5. Accordingly, only brief consideration will be given to these
findings here, with the most notable differences between the surveys being
highlighted (see Parker et al., 1987b for details).

Sex and age   Of the known opioid users, 601 (77 per cent) were male, which
is a male to female ratio of 3.3:1 — compared with 3.9:1 in the first survey
(see Table 3.4). Furthermore, the sex ratio was even lower for new opioid
users — 2.8:1. This suggests that relatively more females had become either
'known' or involved in opioid use over the two years. The age distribution of
known opioid users was similar to that found in the first survey, with 69 per
cent being aged between 16 and 24 years (compared to 75 per cent in 1984–5).

Unemployment and social deprivation   The unemployment rate among
known opioid users available for work was 83 per cent, compared with 87 per
cent a year earlier. Furthermore, as in the first survey, the rate of known
opioid use was significantly correlated with townships' unemployment rates
and other indicators of social deprivation.

Table 3.4 Annual rates of problem drug use and known opioid use in Wirral in 1985–6

Population	Size	Problem drug users		All opioid users		New opioid users	
		N	Rate*	N	Rate*	N	Rate*
Overall	338,952	1,076	3.2	788	2.3	356	1.1
Adults	262,149	1,000	3.8	783	3.0	351	1.3
Males	162,186	811	5.0	601	3.7	259	1.6
Females	176,766	223	1.3	182	1.0	94	0.5
5–15	56,335	76	1.3	5	0.1	5	0.1
16–24	47,706	698	14.6	538	11.3	222	4.7
25–34	45,660	196	4.3	170	3.7	64	1.4
35–44	38,942	31	0.8	22	0.6	14	0.4
45 +	150,444	4	<0.1	1	<0.1	1	<0.1
Unemployed	26,478	523	19.8	446	16.8	145	5.5
males	19,082	419	22.0	352	18.4	110	5.8
females	7,396	103	13.9	93	12.6	35	4.7

*Per 1,000 population

N.B. The numbers/rates by sex, age group and unemployment are underestimates because the sex, age and/or occupational status of some individuals were unknown, and so these individuals are not included in the breakdown. For instance, the occupational status of the 1,076 problem drug users in 1985–6 was not known in 34 per cent of cases, so it can be estimated that the 'true' rate of problem drug use among the unemployed is 30 per 1,000. Population figures are based on 1981 Census statistics; unemployment figures are for May 1985.

Area of residence   The highest rates of known opioid use continued to be found in Birkenhead (8.3 per 1,000) and Ford (7.7 per 1,000), though rates in Woodchurch, Wallasey Village and Moreton, while still high, had dropped substantially since the 1984–5 survey. However, there were also indications that heroin use continued to thrive in such areas as Rock Ferry, New Ferry, Bidston, New Brighton, Tranmere, Bromborough and Liscard. This suggests a geographical diffusion from the more central townships where Wirral's heroin 'epidemic' began towards two areas: south-east towards townships alongside the River Mersey, and north-east to townships in the 'top corner' of Wirral. By contrast, the rates of known opioid use in West Kirby and Heswall, the two main urban townships in Wirral's most middle-class area (Deeside), had dropped considerably — from 3.7 to 1.7 per 1,000 in the former case, and from 3 to 1 per 1,000 in the latter case. Nevertheless, rates of known opioid use among the youth (16–24-year-old) populations were higher than 5 per 1,000 in 23 of Wirral's 48 townships.

Details of heroin use   As in the first survey, over 90 per cent of the opioid users attending Wirral's main two facilities for drug users were daily users of heroin, and had been using heroin for between six months and five years. At the time of their first agency contact, the majority reported that they were using between two 'bags' (about £10) and a gram of heroin (£60) per day, the typical daily quantity reported being 0.25–0.5 gram (between £20 and £35). Of course, the actual quantities of heroin used per day are probably much lower, because street heroin is diluted (adulterated) to varying degrees. Finally, up to one in five heroin users in treatment was regularly or occasionally injecting the drug — 15 per cent of those known to the Drugs Council and 20 per cent of those known to the Detoxification Unit, compared to an overall figure of 12 per cent in the first survey. This implies that there were probably up to 300 injectors among Wirral's known heroin users in 1985-6, enough to make the potential spread of HIV infection in Wirral an issue of major concern.

Conclusions

Changes in the characteristics of heroin users

There were indications of some changes in the characteristics of Wirral's heroin users between 1984 and 1986, such as the higher proportion of females. Rather than speculate on this increase here, the reasons for female involvement in heroin use will be examined more fully in Chapter 4.

As in the first survey, four out of five known opioid users who were available for work were unemployed, and the rate of problem drug use was again significantly correlated with townships' unemployment rates and other indicators of social deprivation. The highest rates of known heroin use continued to be found in Birkenhead and Ford, though there were signs of geographical diffusion toward townships on the Mersey side of Wirral, in both the north and the south. However, it is not possible to accurately chart the spread of heroin use through a community without recourse to more detailed information about new heroin users who are not known to official agencies — the largest group of heroin users, according to research in the USA. The profile of the 'hidden sector' user will be examined in Chapter 5.

As in the first survey, over 90 per cent of the opioid users attending Wirral's main treatment facilities in 1985-6 were daily users of heroin, who had been using heroin for between six months and five years. As already stated, the vast majority were, at the time of their first agency contact, using between two 'bags' and a gram of heroin per day, the typical daily quantity being 0.25-0.5 gram (costing between £20 and £35). The question of how users manage to finance such an expensive habit is examined in Chapter 7.

Finally, up to one in five known heroin users had been injecting the drug during 1985-6, a worrying increase on the previous year. As mentioned earlier, injection is a method of use which creates many more problems than 'chasing the dragon', not least of which is the potential spread of HIV infection. Injectors who become infected through sharing needles can spread the virus to people in the wider community through sexual contacts, particularly those who turn to prostitution as a means of financing the habit. Moreover, it may be occasional injectors, rather than regular injectors, who are the higher-risk group for spreading HIV, since casual injectors may be more inclined to share equipment than regular injectors, who are more likely to have their own 'set of works' and to be aware of safe cleaning procedures.

Problems with forecasting the course of the epidemic

The second survey of the prevalence of problem drug use in Wirral identified 1,076 drug users known to eight official agencies, of whom 788 were opioid users. This was over 500 fewer opioid users than was found during the previous year's survey of ten agencies, and there is still a reduction in numbers of 375 if we compare the figures obtained from the five agencies contacted in both surveys. However, such a basic comparison is too crude to be meaningful. Consequently, a more valid analysis was undertaken, using the formula:

(1985–6 prevalence) = (1984–5 prevalence) –
(20 per cent [estimated] outcidence) + (1985–6 incidence)

As detailed in the previous section, using a theoretical framework developed from American research into heroin 'epidemics', this formula allowed us to estimate that prevalence was still increasing but that incidence was decreasing. Consequently, it was forecast that the prevalence of heroin use might also begin to fall from 1988–9. However, such forecasts about trends in drug-taking behaviour are, of necessity, based on several untested assumptions, and also need to be evaluated in the light of various practical considerations.

Our data were subject to several constraints: a far lower response rate from probation officers in the second survey; the effects of changes in agency policies and practices during the two survey years (e.g. medics' notifying practices, police detection efforts/successes); the 'loss' of some users identified in the first survey, and of some new users, to institutions and agencies not covered by the research (e.g. custody, rehabilitation units, drug agencies in adjacent areas); disillusionment with some agencies among heroin users (particularly medical services), which may have produced a higher ratio of unknown to known users than in the previous year; the optimistic assumption of 20 per cent annual outcidence — for instance, one review of follow-up studies of opioid users suggests that outcidence after one year is typically around 10 per cent, and may only reach 40–50 per cent after ten years, even for those who have received 'treatment' (Home Office 1986, ch. 7); and the decline in the size of the youth population, due largely to the drop in the birth rate during the 1960s — that is, the absolute number of known heroin users could decrease while the rate per 1,000 youths remained the same or even increased (the population figures from which our prevalence rates were calculated derived from 1981 Census statistics, and do not take into account projected trends). Various combinations of these factors could weigh against the surface indications of a decrease in incidence or of an imminent decrease in prevalence.

There are also shortcomings with the theoretical notion that heroin use will eventually 'saturate' the potential user population. First, such a model assumes a static population — that is, it neglects the obvious fact that new generations of school leavers (the age group where use tends to begin) are constantly emerging. Unless we have good reasons for believing that this continuous supply of potential users has somehow become 'inoculated' against heroin use (e.g. through effective drug education), then we have to accept that the concept of total 'saturation' may be implausible. The second problem is that the complex multi-causal nature of drug use makes it difficult to identify what particular combinations of factors make people likely to use heroin, and changes in these causal variables could increase the size of the potential user population. For instance, both of our prevalence surveys found strong correlations between townships' rates of known opioid use and levels of social deprivation, particularly unemployment. Although such correlations do not amount to conclusive evidence of a causal relationship between opioid use and social deprivation, they do indicate a stable association between variations in the two phenomena over time. Consequently, if unemployment and poverty continue to spread into the Wirral population, we can expect a related increase in the number of potential heroin users (cf. Peck and Plant 1986). Two more direct influences on 'susceptibility' that could also forestall any expected decrease in prevalence are changes in the availability, price or purity of heroin or other illicit drugs, and changes in society's response to heroin use. In the former case, one clear example is that if heroin became more easily available and cheaper, more people might begin to take it. In the latter case, the prevalence of heroin use might also remain high if we continue to employ strategies (e.g. mass-media 'fear-arousal' campaigns) for which there is no evidence of effectiveness. For these and other reasons, forecasts of future trends in such complex human behaviours as drug-taking are necessarily conditional and tentative.

The limitations of epidemiology

In conclusion, it should be emphasised that the epidemiology of drug use is a science in its infancy, and that the model of the heroin 'epidemic' briefly presented here contains much 'sophisticated guesswork'. Improvements in our ability to forecast future trends in drug-taking and drug problems greatly depend upon theoretical developments in the social and human sciences, as well as upon the design and proper funding of large-scale, longitudinal research investigations. Nevertheless, glossing over all the numerical details and hypothetical scenarios, it is clear that Wirral had a relatively high rate of problem drug use in the mid-1980s compared with similar areas in other parts of the country, though there are data and arguments to support both the forecast of an ongoing rise in prevalence as well as the prediction of an imminent decline. Even so, our model of heroin 'epidemics' suggested that the rate of growth of the Wirral 'epidemic' was slowing up, and that it would peak during the late 1980s. Indeed, the history of previous heroin 'epidemics' in the USA and the UK suggests both that, on the one hand, this plateau stage will be followed by a slow decline in the prevalence of heroin use, and, on the other hand, that a new heroin 'epidemic' might occur in the late 1990s or at the start of the next century.

However, the nature of the social structures and processes which affect the drug-taking behaviour of the population continue to undergo great changes, and, in the final analysis, the possibility that the prevalence of heroin use in

Wirral will peak but not fall cannot be ruled out. Another distinct possibility is that, although annual incidence appears to be declining, it may stabilise at a far higher endemic level than that characterising the population prior to the 'epidemic' in 1979. The use of legal drugs (alcohol and tobacco) in this century is certainly characterised more by this model than by a bell-shaped curve, despite efforts to control their use. Furthermore, evidence from police convictions and research suggests that the use of cannabis, and perhaps amphetamines, though punctuated by temporary troughs, has increased consistently over the last three decades. Hence, scientific forecasts alone are not enough. Continued monitoring of both the drug users known to official agencies and the 'hidden users' in the community is the only sure way of keeping abreast of developments in drug-taking behaviour. The importance of systematic observation and empirical study is underlined by the additional need to monitor the changing characteristics of drug users, particularly the geographical areas and social groups in which new users appear, and the popularity of injection as a method of using heroin and other drugs.

We mentioned in the Introduction that earlier sociological studies of deviant behaviour provide notes of caution about investigating phenomena like heroin use. These 'interactionist'-type studies have emphasised the importance of social response and reaction in creating or reconstructing social problems through ill-conceived strategies based on 'moral panics'. They suggest that the behaviour of the young is often defined as threatening by adults in positions of power and that, encouraged by media campaigns, the state can often overreact to 'deviant' behaviour and basically make matters worse (Frith 1984; Muncie 1984). Consequently various groups, whether homosexuals or occasional cannabis users, mods or rockers or punks, often become stigmatised and repressed by official responses which are disproportionate to the 'harm', if any, the 'deviants' are being accused of causing.

It might seem that employing a fairly mechanical and impersonal survey approach, as described in this and the previous chapter, is not the best way of creating an interactionist perspective. Instead, it seems, we have relied all too heavily on agency definitions and ignored the users' perspective. Furthermore we may appear, by using an epidemiological approach, to have added to the stigma of heroin use by comparing it with a 'disease'. We do not believe this is the case, however. What we have tried to establish through our agency surveys is a social profile of who uses heroin in the community, how much, how often and whether there are any obvious signs that a heroin habit causes users or others serious problems. If heroin use proves relatively harmless to all concerned then we should advocate legal reform and controlled availability. If in fact very few young people are actually 'into' heroin, then all the media coverage, the 'war on drugs', the setting up of new clinics and drugs squads, is all overreaction and should be stopped in its tracks now. Similarly the moral crusaders, newspaper proprietors and muck-raking journalists should be called off. Finally, such a finding would confirm that the interactionist studies of the 1970s, based primarily on cannabis use, were correct in emphasising the significance of amplification and 'secondary' deviance fostered by inappropriate official responses.

The actual picture to emerge from our surveys is, of course, far from simple, but it does allow us to check out some of the issues. First, it is clear that literally thousands of young people in this community are using heroin regularly (see Chapter 5). The belief amongst the journalists, local state officials and community elders that heroin use is widespread has been confirmed. Heroin use is not a spurious construction of a 'moral panic' but a social reality. Second, heroin use has grown rapidly from a small baseline, and, whilst we shall have to describe the prevalence of heroin use 'hidden' from agencies, particularly in middle-class areas, it is not a long-standing activity suddenly discovered by labellers which is redefined as a problem. Unlike, say, child sexual abuse, a long-standing reality only recently recognised as a major 'problem', heroin use in Wirral has grown and become pathologised simultaneously. Again little support for labelling theory emerges. Third, we are, in part at least, talking about an activity which appears to be defined as problematic by users themselves. A significant minority of our survey subjects referred themselves to the GP, drugs counsellor, and so on. Clearly we need to differentiate between the problematic nature of heroin itself as against the 'hassle' caused by its illegality, impurity and uneven availability. It is not clear from the survey findings whether heroin *is* potentially a source of real 'primary' problems. This is important and it is an issue which we will address in the coming chapters as we attempt to separate out the problems for both users and their community and whether the source of the problem is with heroin use or its legal and social status.

In conclusion, our epidemiological surveys have allowed an aerial view of heroin use in an English community. We have taken snap-shots through time and from sufficient height to gain a panoramic view which shows that meaningful patterns are at work. We know what is happening, on the surface at least, with some certainty, although only time will tell whether our forecasts will prove correct. We also know that socio-economic variables play a potentially vital role in the patterns of drug use. In short, we know *what* is happening but not *why*. We will not find out why unemployment and heroin use are connected, why large groups of young men and women have taken on heroin use for the first time, or how they get the street money, without talking to them. Nor will notions of contagion and suspectibility be on the agenda when we meet them. People, as we will see and know already (see Stewart 1987), largely *choose* to take heroin and *decide* to take on the lifestyle associated with it.

The next three chapters concentrate on interviews with users themselves and on establishing the extent to which our agency surveys, which define the known sector of drug use, underestimate the overall prevalence of drug taking in the community.

Note

1 Outcidence is a term suggested by Jason Ditton (Glasgow University), which we have developed. We do not know of any previous usage of this term.

4

Talking to known users

During the course of the research programme, a total of 125 heroin users were interviewed. For the first stage of the field work, a random sample was taken from the client lists of the two agencies that provided the team with the most systematic and varied information on users, that is, the local Detoxification Unit and Drugs Council. A profile of the 'drug career' patterns of this 'known' user group will be presented in this chapter. The second stage of the field work involved contacting 'hidden' heroin users, that is, those who had not come into contact with Wirral agencies. To achieve this, the interviewees of the first stage were used as the basis of a series of 'snowball' samples from the 'hidden' sector. The results of this second stage will be detailed in Chapter 5.

The concept of the 'drug career' has been used by a number of authors (for example, Becker 1963) to systematise the response patterns of individuals who have come into contact with a given drug. The importance of this way of conceptualising drug use lies in its ability to treat drug use non-judgementally as a continuing process which can and does vary between individuals and through time for the same individual.

It is important to note here that the drug career patterns of 'known' users presented below cannot be representative of the total user population. Firstly, users tend to contact agencies one to three years after starting to use heroin and, secondly, interviews took place over 12 months after their first contact with the two agencies concerned. Consequently, the sample group had been using heroin for an average of five years when they were interviewed. Given that these 'older' users are more likely to have worked and to inject heroin, rather than smoke it, the sample is skewed away from the archetypal 'young unemployed heroin chaser' profiled in our prevalence surveys.

Methodology

A random sample of 100 was taken from the 308 patients who had been
referred to the local Detoxification Unit during the same 12 months of the first
prevalence study period. A similar sample of 100 was taken from the 216
clients who received counselling from the local Drugs Council. Response
sheets were sent out to these 200 with a covering letter from the agency
concerned and 85 positive responses were received. In addition, 24 response
sheets were returned because the user had changed address and could not be
contacted either by the agency concerned and/or the user's family. In one
instance, a response sheet was returned with a statement to the effect that the
person had come off heroin and did not wish to be involved with anything
concerning drugs ever again, including our own project. In 90 cases, no reply
was received. In all, 61 respondents were eventually contacted and
interviewed, 28 were Detoxification Unit patients and 39 were Drugs Council
clients, six individuals having been selected by both samples.

The interviews were designed to collect basic biographical details relating to
the age, sex, employment profile, housing conditions, etc., of the user; to outline
the characteristics of the user's 'drug career' so as to construct a typology of
users and to assess whether there was any particular stage in a given career where it
would be possible to target a user for treatment or intervention; and, to ask
users to assess their experience of local statutory and voluntary drugs services.
Initially, it was decided to conduct short unstructured interviews in order to
collect basic data concerning the issues outlined above and to follow up with
in-depth interviews at a later date. However, given the readiness of our
subjects to talk at length about their drug use, the time limits placed on the
research, and the possibility of a number of informants being sentenced
and/or convicted before the second interview took place, it quickly became
clear that the majority of interviewees would probably be seen only once and
that in-depth interviews should be conducted on first contact, if that suited the
informant.

Interviewing took place in the respondent's home when possible. This
occurred in 50 cases. Five interviewees were in custody at the time of the
interview (two in prison, one in detention centre, and two on remand) and six
preferred to be interviewed outside the family home (four at the Drugs Council
and two in a local community centre) principally to prevent their families from
finding out about their habit. The interviews began with a chat about the aims
of the research project, emphasising the importance of the 'consumer's point of
view' for the assessment of future service provision in Wirral. Following
this, and usually beginning with 'How did you get into smack in the first
place?', the interviewer then proceeded through a list of questions to be
answered, not in any ordered fashion, but in a conversational manner allowing
the respondent to move in whichever direction he or she wanted. The
interviewer only 'butted in' when clarification was required on a specific topic
or if the conversation wandered too far off the point. In only a handful of cases
did the interviewer have to direct the interview to any great extent, and then

only in cases where the informant responded only in short phrases. In four instances, the interviewees refused to discuss their criminal activities as these concerned crimes for which they had not been convicted.

Social profile of interviewees

The sample group consisted of 18 females and 43 males. Their age at interview varied from 17 to 36, giving an average age of about 24 for both females and males. The majority were single (62 per cent), and living in rented, mainly council, accommodation (72 per cent). Few had any educational qualifications or trade skills that could be sold on the shrinking job market. One had A levels, three had O levels, six had CSEs and the rest (84 per cent) had no qualifications at all.

While 42 (69 per cent) interviewees had worked at some time or other, the overwhelming majority (89 per cent) were unemployed at the time of interview. The length of unemployment ranged from a matter of months to over ten years, the average being between three and four years. Nineteen of the interviewees (31 per cent) had never worked since leaving school. The rest had worked in a variety of occupations, principally manual or unskilled, such as shop assistant and labourer. For six of these (24 per cent) the duration of their last job was less than 12 months and for the group as a whole the average was less than 17 months.

Seventy-two per cent of those who had previously worked were currently unemployed as a direct result of their heroin use: 17 were dismissed for continual lateness and/or absenteeism; two were dismissed for theft from work to finance their habit; two lost their jobs when they were imprisoned for burglary or possession of heroin; one was dismissed after two years of illness related to his drug use; and one went bankrupt trying to support his habit. A further seven (22 per cent) had been employed on a short-term basis only, on government training schemes. Of the rest, one left voluntarily because he was bored with his job, and one because of her pregnancy. In three instances the reason for unemployment was not given. In short, the single most significant factor in the unemployed status of those who had previously worked had been their use of heroin.

The 'negative' consequences of recreational drug use have been well documented in the Press, the image of the 'drop out' immediately springing to mind. However, the drug use of the interview group needs to be placed in its wider social context. In the first instance, apart from the use of heroin itself, the social profile of the sample group does not differ significantly from that of Wirral's working-class youth, who also share high unemployment, absence of educational qualifications and a lack of marketable labour skills. Secondly, as we have shown in Chapter 2, there are consistent, significant, positive correlations between the rates of known opioid use on Wirral and the six major indicators of social deprivation: unemployment, council tenancies, overcrowding, large families, unskilled labour force, and presence of single parents.

While an analysis of individual psychological traits may be important in treating an individual user, these can only help to explain why that given individual 'got hooked'. It is only by reference to the contribution of 'environment', both social and physical, to the spread of heroin use that conclusions might be drawn as to why heroin use reached 'epidemic' proportions in such a short space of time in the Wirral area.

Starting off

This section will address itself to the two fundamental questions identified by Feldman (1986) in his discussion of 'heroin epidemics' and locate them in the Wirral context. Firstly, why, in the absence of any generalised heroin use prior to 1979 on Wirral, did large numbers of young people suddenly start experimenting with heroin? Secondly, once the first 'wave' of users passed and the physical and social consequences of their habit became visible to the Wirral population at large, why did the incidence of heroin use continue to climb?

Historical context

First of all, we need to look at the history of opioid use in Wirral. The field interviews with users reveal that, before the current outbreak, there were only a few isolated 'pockets' of opioid users in Wirral. These were mainly intravenous injectors who first experimented with drugs in the late 1960s and early 1970s. Their intake was not restricted to heroin, but often covered the whole range of opioids, both synthetic and natural, as well as a variety of other drugs such as cannabis, hallucinogenics and stimulants. Their small numbers and low profile, combined with a 'hippie' ethos of 'peace and love' to which crimes involving the burglary of people's homes and violence against the person are anathema, meant that this group had little impact on the community as a whole. The criminal activity of these older users was in the main restricted to offences relating to the possession and supply of the drugs themselves and the burglary of chemists' premises to obtain drugs.

Then, during the late 1970s, Wirral GPs began prescribing large amounts of opioids such as Diconal and Palfium. These are moderate to severe pain relievers, but numerous instances were cited in the interviews where GPs had prescribed them for relatively minor ailments, some of which were fictitious, such as headaches, backache and arthritis. What is also significant is that prescriptions for these opioids were often for large amounts — 50 or 100 at a time. In the words of one user, 'they were giving them out as if they were going out of style'. Obviously, GPs who prescribed in this manner became the target for those already using other drugs, including the older heroin users who knew that, when crushed and injected, these drugs gave a 'better hit' than heroin.

At more or less the same time, a heroin injector from Liverpool, who had also been dealing to finance his own habit, moved house to one of Wirral's more affluent townships and began dealing in heroin on a large scale — in ounces and half-ounces. His clients were mainly older heroin users from the late 1960s and early 1970s who, in their turn, sold grams to those 'new' opioid users, that is, pot smokers and 'pill poppers', who had been 'turned on' in the late 1970s with the unwitting help of their GPs. This group then began distributing 'bags' around the housing estates. That the bulk of the first new wave of Wirral's heroin users obtained heroin from a single source might seem startling. However, interviews in the field, including those with some eight middle-ranking heroin dealers living in different Wirral townships, verify this fact. Moreover the same pattern has been identified elsewhere (Hughes 1977). In Chapter 7 we discuss how, once initiated, incidence spreads from township to township and via personal relationships within the illicit economy.

To summarise, Wirral began the 1980s with a steady flow of opioids available from both legal and street sources and it was at this time that the majority of Wirral's users began their habit. In terms of the 61 users in the sample who were interviewed, the years in which they first used heroin ranged from 1969 to 1984. However, almost 94 per cent were initiated into heroin use between 1979 and 1984, that is, during the current 'epidemic'. Having introduced the 'supply side' of the equation, it remains to account for the pattern of the 'demand'. The interviews identified a variety of entries into heroin use, based, first, on the relationship between the initiate and the person who introduced him or her to the drug, that is, the social 'how?'; and, secondly, on the reasons given by the users themselves as to why they took heroin in the first place, that is, the personal 'why?'.

Social routes into heroin use

The way a person comes into contact with heroin, is offered it, and accepts it, is intimately related to the heroin use of the significant others in that person's life. That is to say, heroin use does not come 'out of the blue'; people are initiated into it via social mechanisms that include ideologies as to what constitutes acceptable and unacceptable behaviour. Approximately 65 per cent of the interviewees were introduced to heroin by a close friend or workmate; 20 per cent, mostly women, by their partner; 10 per cent by their regular dealer of other drugs; and 5 per cent by a member of the family. Thus, contrary to the mythology propagated by the 'popular' Press, these user histories point to the fact that, at street level, heroin use is more likely to spread along friendship and family networks (90 per cent), than via the 'evil pusher' (10 per cent) (see also Pearson 1987).

The variety of relationships between the novice and the introducer is clearly differentiated along gender lines. On the one hand, while two-thirds of the females were introduced to heroin by their male partner, that is, husband or boyfriend, none of the males were introduced to it by their female partner. Similarly, whereas 28 per cent of female interviewees were introduced by a close female friend, 81 per cent of males were introduced by a close male friend. These differences are related to the wider patterns of drug use in society at large in which females are proportionately less likely to engage in recreational drug use then males, as this and a number of earlier studies show (for example, Belle and Goldman 1980). This was verified by the interviewees when they were asked how many of their close friends, of the same sex as themselves, used heroin during the prevalence study period. Females stated that an average of 1.8 of their 'five best friends' also used heroin, while male informants gave an average of 4.3. In part, this pattern is also related to the fact that the females in the study group were generally older than the males. They were, therefore, more likely to have a regular partner, to have less contact with former friends, and to be spending the greatest proportion of their time fulfilling a traditional domestic role. In addition, as will be shown later, it is the male in a given relationship who more frequently engages in criminal activity to support the couple's habit than the female. In short, the probability is that women will more often gain access to heroin through a male, frequently via a 'romantic relationship', than any other social route.[1]

Motivation

Following from this we turn to the 'motivation factor'. All the interviewees were asked what moved them to experiment with heroin in the first instance. The largest group (33 per cent) first tried heroin out of curiosity which, in most of the cases, had been aroused by the previous use of other drugs. One interviewee stated:

> I just wanted to see what it was all about. I mean, we'd used other drugs and got a good hit and we just wanted to try smack to see what it was like.

A further 5 per cent began to use heroin as 'a change' from their usual drug. This group, all known to each other, were daily injectors of 'speed' and made a conscious decision to change to what they thought was a 'less dangerous drug'. As one member of this small group observed:

> I'd started to get into a bit of a mess with speed. You can't describe the paranoia. For the years we were taking speed, we wouldn't go into a pub or a crowded room. We had started fixing it by then and were hallucinating and everything so we thought we'll stop taking speed and take smack instead.

Another closely related motivation factor which occurred in 15 per cent of all cases was the interviewee's prior addiction to an opioid other than heroin, principally Diconal. In the words of one former Diconal user:

> As I said, I did me shoulder in and it was really bad and me mam got some dikes off me gran who had arthritis and I felt great. I felt so good that I decorated the hall. Anyway, I started hitting doctors for dikes after that and then, when this smack started coming around, it was easier to get hold of than dikes.

Here, the move occurred when Diconal became less readily available, after 1982, precisely the time when the supply of heroin in Wirral began to rise. For these three groups, then, their previous drug use has acted as a 'gateway' to further drug use. It is only amongst the third, however, that this can be seen as 'causal' in any determinate sense. With reference to prior drug use, excluding alcohol and tobacco, most of the sample (92 per cent) had regularly used at least one other drug for recreational purposes prior to taking heroin. (Only five, four female and one male, stated that their initiation into drug use involved heroin itself.) The age at which this 'secondary' drug use began varied between 13 and 24, although 82 per cent of these individuals were concentrated in the lower age band of 13–17. Nineteen had used only one drug prior to heroin use, principally cannabis, the rest using a variety of drug combinations. Of importance here is the fact that 14 interviewees (23 per cent) were regular users of another opioid, principally Diconal, eight of them on a daily basis. Whilst some of these drugs may have been obtained by illegal means, the evidence suggests that a significant minority became addicted to opioids originating from a legal source, that is, family practitioners.

The motivation factor for a further 21 per cent of the interviewees was the heroin use of the majority of their friends — sometimes loosely described as 'peer-group pressure'. The 'pressure' in these cases was both internal, with individuals feeling the need to conform to what had become the 'norm' in their social group, and also external, with individuals being urged to conform and, given the nature of heroin use, subsequently excluded from the group if they did not. Again, for reasons stated above, this group was differentiated along gender lines, occurring in none of the female cases and 30 per cent of the male cases. A typical response from this group was:

> We just used to hang around with each other and it was just one of those things, like, that you'd never done before. We got into pot at the same time, we got into acid at the same time and then there was more smack around than pot, so we got into that.

A further 15 per cent, all female, stated that the major factor in their experimentation was their male partner's use. This does not mean that women are reduced to merely playing a passive role in their initiation, a point made by Rosenbaum (1981) in her study of female addicts in the USA. It is simply the case that the heroin use of the male partner places her in a situation in which the drug is not only readily available, but its use is also seen as socially acceptable. It is from within this situation that the female then decides whether to use it or not. As one young woman remarked:

> Just curiosity really. Well, me husband got into it before me. He used to have a wrap of his own and he'd give it to me when he went out. He used to play pool and that. Anyway, I was using it behind his back. It was just 'cos it was around, y'know.

The remaining eight interviewees, all male, played a somewhat passive role in their initiation. Five went to their usual dealer to buy cannabis or speed and, as there was a drought on at the time, were offered and accepted heroin instead. As one stated:

> It just took over from the lack of draw on the estate. I was at a stage where I was used to getting something like cannabis or whatever and, with none of that being around, I thought a bit of this won't do me any harm and it just took off from there.

Two others were offered it by their usual dealer. One was regularly given a 'chase' while he waited for his cannabis to be weighed out and so was initiated. The other worked as a 'runner' or delivery man, for a large dealer and was paid out in heroin to the tune of 2 grams a day which he began to consume. Finally, one other began to use heroin almost by default in that he and a friend bought heroin with the specific aim of selling it for a profit. This was before the 'epidemic' had reached its current proportions and, being unsuccessful in their enterprise, they used it rather than throw it away.

An additional important facilitating factor, although not specific to Wirral, was the possibility of smoking heroin, 'chasing the dragon'. Had it been essential to inject, many 'new' users stated that they would probably not have experimented with heroin in the first place. This was the experience of the following informant:

> I think it was being able to chase. It didn't seem as heavy as injecting. I wasn't really keen on injecting because of the name that it'd got. So that's how I got into it, really.

It is interesting to note that a number of new users, rather than inject, snorted heroin as they previously had done with speed and coke until they saw a television programme on Hong Kong which 'instructed' them how to chase the dragon. In addition, given that they had little, if any, social contact with the 'older' user group, there was little street wisdom about the consequences of heroin use. On the one hand, myths abounded about the non-addictive nature of heroin when 'chased'. On the other hand, few had witnessed another user undergoing withdrawal symptoms. By the time the 'first wave' of new users began to 'turkey' themselves some six to 18 months after their initiation, they were daily users. As to succeeding 'waves', it would seem that curiosity and peer-group pressure, together with other social factors such as drug availability, overcame any reservations they might have had regarding addiction and withdrawal. A significant proportion of these younger interviewees, both male and female, simply ignored the knowledge beginning to accumulate. When pressed on this point, a typical response was: 'Why not? There's nothing else to do anyway except spend all day watching the telly.'

This complex of supply and demand factors led to the current 'epidemic' in Wirral, and its spread to the majority of Wirral's townships. However, whilst it might be stating the obvious, the overriding factor in this situation has been the sudden influx and continuing constant supply of heroin at an 'affordable' price. To paraphrase an old saying, the water has to be there for the horse to be able to drink. The following section will demonstrate how the drug careers of the interviewees developed following this initial stage.

A continuing career

Obviously, the length of time between first use and second use and, subsequently, between first use and daily use, is intimately related to a number of personal and social factors. It is important to note that not all those who dabble in heroin become daily or even 'regular' users. However, as the sample was selected from those who had sought treatment or counselling for their daily habit, such users are necessarily excluded from this study.

Becoming a daily user

For over three-quarters of the sample group (61 per cent of females and 81 per cent of males), the time lag between the first experimentation with heroin and second use was less than one month. Nineteen (31 per cent) of these interviewees (four females and 15 males) used heroin for a second time less than one week after first use. For a further 20 per cent, the gap was between one month and six months and for the remaining 5 per cent it was over six months.

In terms of this initial time lapse, two distinct groups can be identified. On the one hand, there are those individuals whom we shall call the 'career' users, those who were already daily users of another opioid or amphetamine sulphate. Here, second use came quickly, a matter of hours rather than days or months. For these, while the desire to experience a 'hit' was important, the overriding factor in second use was the 'need' to keep withdrawal symptoms at bay. As one user explained:

> I'd been banging up dikes for a couple of years when smack came on the scene and I just sort of carried on as I had been doing, y'know, with the smack instead of the dike. You get a different hit, like. I'd rather have the hit off dikes anyday, but smack was easier to get hold of, so I got into that instead.

On the other hand, there are what might be termed the 'recreational' users, those who were still in the 'experimental' stage. Here, second use depended more on hedonism, the desire to experience the 'hit'. It is interesting that a large proportion of these 'new' users experienced some unpleasantness on first use such as vomiting and dizziness. In one instance, a young female was so ill that she did not use heroin again for another 18 months. For the rest, the euphoria that they experienced more than matched the unpleasantness. Interviewees typically said things like 'It was an incredible buzz', 'I felt great', 'It made me forget everything else'.

The time lags between first use and daily use show a similar distribution, with 72 per cent of interviewees becoming daily users within a period of six months after initial use. For almost 20 per cent of the sample, daily use came less than one week after first use. This group of 12 included nine of the 'career' users, that is, seven daily opioid users and two daily speed users, two women whose male partners were dealing in heroin, and one young employed male. For eight of the interviewees, daily use came between one week and one month later. Two were 'career' users, one of opioids and one of speed; one woman's husband was a dealer; two other women began to steal from their husband's 'stash' without his knowledge; two were unemployed; and one had been left a small legacy just prior to his heroin use. Daily use for the others came between one month and over 18 months later. The onset of daily use, then, is related to two main factors: firstly, 'need', as in the case of the 'career' users; secondly, 'access', as in those cases of 'recreational' use where heroin was readily available, or where finance did not present a problem.

It must be remembered that, for all but the 'career' users, the daily quantity of heroin administered during this early period was generally relatively small. The typical interviewee profile of the 'recreational user' is that of 'dabbling' at weekends, usually sharing a 'bag' with a friend, then gradually filling in the days in between until they are all taken up by heroin use. In the words of one young male user:

> And for the next three or four months, I was just getting it of a weekend. I'd just get a couple of bags for a Saturday night or whatever and then eventually I just got into it deeper and deeper.

Even at the start of the daily stage, apart from the exceptions noted, it was rare to find anyone using more than one or two 'bags' a day, that is, a habit of between £5 and £10 a day. Such a habit was 'affordable' by those in work, those who were perhaps already engaged in petty crime, and those who were relying on the legal or illegal activity of others to support their use.

A career of limited options

During these initial stages of their drug career, changes in the lifestyle of the majority of the sample were minimal. Those who had been previously addicted to opioids could perceive no changes whatsoever. Their daily routine was already totally centred on the obtaining and consuming of drugs. For the rest, lifestyle changes in the main concerned their social activity. Two distinct paths can be identified here. For one group, the social options available to the user actually expanded, at least in the early stages. This was the case with the small group who had been daily injectors of speed. This group had isolated themselves socially because of the paranoia that they experienced as a side-effect of their drug use. It was also the case for a small number of women with children who felt isolated because their social horizons were constrained by domestic and family expectations. Heroin use for these individuals meant a broadening of social contact. For the rest, their social options were generally diminished. In the case of those who worked, non-working hours were utilised 'scoring' and using smack, rather than meeting friends or family. Similarly, the unemployed found the focus of their social circle also becoming centred on heroin. However, most of the interviewees stated that they did not perceive this process taking place. As one young male observed:

> I was that busy, y'know, getting up, going out to score, having a toot, going out again to score, that I didn't even realise what was going on. It just crept up on me.

As their heroin use continued, it was generally the case that consumption increased. At the 'height' of their career, the sample group used an average of between 0.25 and 0.5 gram a day, a daily habit costing between £20 and £35. This is not to suggest a unilinear path of ever-increasing usage. The quantity administered at any given time was determined by a whole range of factors, causing it to oscillate greatly. Once daily use had set in, the user's principal concern was to obtain sufficient heroin to keep withdrawal symptoms at bay. Anything more than this was treated as a 'bonus'. A typical response to a question concerning the quantity used was:

> It's not like that, really. You just use what you can get hold of. It's up and down all the time. Y'know, you have good days and bad days. No matter how much you've got, you use it all. Whether I had a bag or a gram, I'd still have nothing left for in the morning.

The question of quantity used is obviously intimately related to the way a given individual finances his or her habit, a perspective which will be taken up in Chapter 7.

It was at this moment of increasing daily use that the most profound lifestyle changes were perceived by the interviewees. Many stated it was also the point at which they 'realised' they were addicted. As one user put it:

> It took me about three months, perhaps longer, three to six months before I realised that I was dependent on it. The first time I was strung out I didn't know what it was. I felt ill and someone gave me some DFs and I felt better.

The majority of those who were working lost their jobs for the reasons already detailed above. Those who remained in work found that their non-working hours totally revolved around their heroin use:

> It takes a lot of time scoring and that, y'know, you've got no time for anything else. It just takes up all your life really. With me working, by the time you got home from work, it'd be 5 o'clock. It might take you till 9 o'clock at night to score some nights. You're sort of running around all the time, so you don't get time for anything else.

In social terms, users tended to lose their old friends as they became more deeply involved in the smack subculture. This was more the experience of females than males because, as has already been noted, more of the males' friends also used heroin. While not stated overtly by most interviewees, although some were asked specifically about this, there was a tendency to use the word 'friend' to signify a pre-heroin relationship, whereas phrases such as 'this guy I know' and 'a bloke who lives around the corner' were used to describe a post-heroin use relationship even though the user might be spending a great deal of time with that person on a daily basis. One user commented:

> You don't have friends when you're a smackhead. All you're worried about is when you're gonna get your next hit.

The move to injecting

During this period of social upheaval, a significant minority moved from 'chasing' to injecting. Almost 20 per cent, the longer-term 'career' users, had injected heroin from the start. However, by the time of interview, another 13 per cent had made the transition to daily injecting. On the one hand, having been 'on the scene' for some time, they were more likely to have come into contact with other injectors. On the other hand, they had also reached a point where they were using sufficient quantities that injecting, which requires less heroin for a 'better hit', became 'attractive' enough to overcome any anxieties they had previously felt. As one former injector stated:

> I started off by smoking it and then, when I injected it, I found I got more of a hit, y'know what I mean. It lasted longer and it was a better hit as well.

When injecting heroin or amphetamines intravenously, users experience a 'rush', a sudden surge, rather than a slow build-up. The drug enters the blood stream directly, absorption begins almost immediately and, thus, the time gap between being 'straight' and 'high' is relatively short. In the words of one interviewee:

> We got into injecting speed almost right away 'cos of the rush. It's like a train hitting you. It was the same when we got into smack. Once you've injected for any length of time, there's no point in snorting or chasing. I mean if you're into the hit, you've got to inject then, otherwise you're just using it to keep the turkey away.

Learning to inject is a necessarily hazardous process. Whereas the older 'career' users served their 'apprenticeship' at a time when the majority of users also injected, this fund of knowledge was not readily available to the new users. The majority were introduced to injection by a casual acquaintance. This was the experience of one interviewee:

> It was this guy I met in a café. He asked me if I wanted any gear and I said yeah, like. So he took me back to his place and pulled his pants down and took out this big bundle with the works in it, like. I said: 'What's going on here?', and he said: 'This is how I use it, like'. So I hit it up and thought: 'This is alright'.

Of particular significance, given the current concern about AIDS, is the fact that almost 70 per cent of the whole sample group had injected at least once prior to interview with many of these being 'casual' injectors, that is, chasing daily, but injecting occasionally, for example, at parties. Obviously, injecting on such a casual basis, given the fact that the majority will necessarily not possess their own 'works', presents a serious problem in terms of the spread of the HIV infection. Some of these casual injectors do not inject street heroin because of the impurities that it might contain and limit their injecting to other opioids generally stolen from chemist shops. This was the case with the following interviewee:

I've never really been into fixing heroin. I have a couple of times, like when one of me friends brought some home on a ship from Thailand or somewhere. It was about 80 per cent pure and you know there's no rubbish in it. Apart from that, I only crack chemmy gear or else things like dikes and Tuinal.

This was not the response of the majority, however, and the willingness of users to inject dirty drugs and reuse and share equipment represents a major health hazard, which will be discussed in Chapter 9.

Crises for family life

It was also at this stage of increasing daily use and possibly injecting that family relationships generally became strained and in many cases reached breaking point. As was noted earlier, over two-thirds of the study group were single and a large proportion of these were still living in the parental home. Obviously, the heroin use of their son or daughter came as a great shock to most parents, many of whom seem to have had little or no idea that their offspring was involved in any drug use whatsoever, let alone daily heroin use.

In many cases, knowledge of that heroin use came from a third party, particularly the police following the arrest of the user for drug-related offences including burglary and shoplifting. In several instances, the parents gradually became aware that something was 'wrong': the user's physical appearance deteriorated over a period of time; household and personal items were unexplainedly missing from the home; the user began borrowing heavily and often from parents and siblings. Sometimes it was a combination of these factors, as occurred in the following case:

> Well, I'd started going down the nick. I was dead thin and not eating anything and then I got sacked for gross misconduct, y'know, for never going in and that. Me mam must have known something was up, but she didn't really click what it was. It wasn't like it is now. All you see in the papers now is smack, like. Anyway, then I was picked up by the bizzies for possession and it all came out then. That's how they found out.

In approximately half of the cases, the parent found out more directly: either the user told his or her parents, usually at a crisis point in the user's career, for example, when undergoing 'turkey' during a time of drought; or the parent found direct evidence of drug use, such as burnt scraps of tin foil, and confronted the user with this. As one interviewee explained:

> I mainly used to chase it in me mate's house, but sometimes when I got home, I'd have a toot before I went to bed. And me mam found some gear and burnt foil and that was it.

The reaction of parents to this knowledge varied from throwing the user out of the family home to paying for their habit until a place at a treatment centre could be found (see Dorn and South 1987). In two cases, the user was locked in a bedroom for days at a time. The following user describes the dilemma that faced his parents:

Well, she was devastated and me dad. They didn't know what was going on. Whether to lock me in me room, or let me out and do what I wanted to do. In the end, like, I just didn't come back here for a couple of months. I just stayed out, kipping at me mates and that.

In many instances, the first reaction of parents was to take the user along to see the family doctor. It was generally at this time that the user began to think about 'coming off' and the, usually long, association with the various medical and social agencies began.

Coming off and staying off

There is no simple pattern to drugs careers, and these careers end or not (Stimson and Oppenheimer 1982) in divergent ways. Whilst the medical literature refers to 'recovery' and 'relapse', the sociological literature talks of users 'maturing out' of the drugs lifestyle. Whatever the language, the epidemiologists' curves illustrated in Chapter 3 do suggest that the majority of the new users will eventually give up daily heroin use. The motivational accounts of the sample of relatively long-term users suggest the same trend. What is not and cannot yet be clear, is whether this forecasted process will actually occur for the vast majority of Wirral users or whether a large endemic user population will remain in place for the foreseeable future.

The point at which a user comes to the decision to 'kick the habit' is determined by a variety of factors: personal, social and environmental. Most of the sample group (82 per cent) had been using for over two years before they first sought treatment. It is probable, therefore, that there will be a similar time lag between first use and requests for treatment from those within subsequent 'new waves' of users who decide to try and come off.

Practically all the interviewees had made at least one and frequently several attempts to come off. As will be shown, sometimes these were half-hearted, the result of external pressure, rather than personal commitment. However, these should not be considered as 'failures', but part of the learning process during which the user, first, comes to terms with his or her dependency and, second, sets about finding out which is the appropriate path to take. In the words of one female who had been 'detoxed' on a number of occasions:

Well, I don't think I was really ready to come off before. I've come off seven times now. Well, every time I come off it, or get back into it, I've learned something new about meself, like. Each time, like, I've learned not to do this because that's what got me back into it the last time. Seven time, that's a lot of times, y'know, to go back, get off, go back again and get off, but, like, I think I've learned me lesson.

Making the decision

Given the significance of regular heroin use, the psychological and physical dependency often associated with the drug, and the all-embracing nature of the lifestyle usually required to secure funds and supplies, users tend to live from moment to moment and find little time for reflecting upon their situation. It is not easy for users to 'step outside' and take an objective look at their predicament. In the words of one interviewee:

> You're just too busy. If you're not robbing, you're selling what you've robbed, or getting stoned out of your mind. You just don't get time to think. Time just zooms. You don't know where it's gone. The only important thing is how to get your next hit.

In addition, while still involved in this lifestyle, the user rarely regards heroin itself as a problem. When discussing the principal problems affecting their lives, interviewees mainly pointed to the 'hassles' of financing their habit and of obtaining supplies. In only two instances were the 'need to use heroin' and the 'fear of withdrawal' cited as the overriding problem in that person's life. As one user explains:

> It's just the crap that you've got to go through to get a hit, y'know, burgling, scoring and that. I mean, if there was a free supply of smack, I wouldn't have a problem in the world.

Furthermore, there is a general fear of becoming 'known' to the authorities. Myths abound in the heroin community as to the meaning of 'notification' and 'registration' and it is generally assumed that all 'official' agencies are in league with one another. In terms of female users, this can be particularly tragic as in the following case, where the woman did not seek treatment because she assumed that this would eventually lead to the placing of a care order on her children:

> That's why I kept putting it off to go to the doctor to get help 'cos I thought that, with me having kids, he would automatically ring the social services and tell them.

It is not surprising, then, that most of the interviewees first came to the decision to seek help as a direct result of some external influence. This impetus originated mainly from two previously noted sources: the user's immediate family and the police. In the majority of cases, parents or partner persuaded the user to seek help in the form of treatment and/or counselling. This frequently involved coercion, for instance, parents forcibly taking their son or daughter to see the family doctor and wives threatening to leave home and take the children with them. As one interviewee explained:

> I used to smoke as much smack as I could lay me hands on. At one time I was going through two grams a day. I was using for about three years altogether. I had no veins left. All the veins had closed up in me arms and legs and me feet and groin as well. It was when I asked [my wife] to inject me in the neck that she said that she'd leave me and take the [four] kids with her, if I didn't do something about it. Anyway, she phoned the hospital and made an appointment for me and that was that.

In a significant number of other cases, the user was arrested for either possession of illegal drugs or a crime related to financing the habit. Here, two scenarios presented themselves. On the one hand, arrest may have been followed by a term of remand and then imprisonment. Where this occurred, the user was immediately, depending on his point of view, either forced into or presented with the opportunity of detoxing. This did not usually involve medication as the following interviewee's experience of Detention Centre illustrates:

> They don't give you nothing. They just throw you in a white room, just a room with a white floor, white roof, white door. You can't think of anything else but white. No windows as well, just big white lights.

On the other hand, with the prospect of a court case looming, several interviewees felt it was pragmatic to seek help, from their GP or the local Drugs Council, in the hope that this would act as a mitigating factor in sentencing:

> My wife was inside for possession and I had custody of the two kids. I'd got nicked for burglary and, so, the only way to get out of it was by trying the hospital. Get the social services on my side, get the probation on my side. Show them that I'm willing to come off it and hopefully they'll bail me out. So, I gets up to Liverpool Crown Court and all the reports say this man is drug-free. He's drug-free, he's just been to hospital, y'know, he's got the kids, if he goes away, the kids'll end up in a home, which was the biggest factor really. So Judge —— gave us a 21-month suspended sentence and let me walk out the court. Which was great on the day, y'know. I got out, the kids didn't go in a home, and I was still using.

These motivational accounts are both complex and important. Clearly if users present for treatment in 'bad faith', that is, they do not really want to try to come off but are being either coerced or attempting to deceive 'authority', then it is unlikely treatment will succeed. Moreover, most users who did actually want to come off were reacting, not to heroin itself but the associated dangerous and stressful lifestyle. Individuals in this group typically stated that they had become 'sick of the life' or they had come to 'hate smack'. One user summed it up as follows:

> You just get to the point where you are sick and tired of the life that you are living. All the hassles. You've really got to hate heroin to come off. Otherwise you're just wasting your time. Things just gradually start to build up and get on top of you and you either get more into the gear and try to forget about it, or you stop using it and try and sort out what's left of your life.

Thus the way in which a particular individual came to the decision to seek help has an important bearing on what happens subsequently. However, for the user to come off, there should ideally be a suitable treatment regime available.

Getting the treatment

The first person the majority of the sample (90 per cent) turned to for help was the family practitioner. It was the GP who then decided whether to treat the patient, to refer the patient on to another agency, or to do nothing. Given that most of the interviewee group had been using heroin for between four and five years, most had contacted their GP, and frequently several different GPs, on a number of occasions. The group as a whole had contacted a GP regarding their heroin use on over 200 occasions. The way they were dealt with, which varied considerably, depended on a variety of factors, both personal and medical. In this section, we can only provide a brief glimpse of the user patient's perception of the role of the doctor (remembering that by 1987 GPs were becoming very reluctant to treat heroin use at all).

Where GPs offered treatment, two options were generally available, both of which involved the use of another drug usually accompanied by counselling either by the GPs themselves or, more frequently, by a voluntary counselling agency. The two main drugs prescribed by GPs, sometimes concurrently, to the sample group were methadone, a synthetic opioid, and benzodiazepines, principally Valium. Methadone was normally prescribed on a reducing basis. That is, users are given smaller and smaller daily amounts of the drug until they are presumably weaned off opioids altogether. The length of the methadone reduction regime varied considerably, from one week to three months. Obviously, the size of the user's habit and the predisposition of the GP were major factors in this. The prescribing of benzodiazepines was similarly varied. Here, Valium was prescribed not to substitute heroin as such, but rather to help the user overcome problems related to withdrawal, principally sleeplessness.

As has already been noted, because of their introspective lifestyle, many users find it difficult to step back and assess their situation objectively. It is possible, therefore, that in reply to questions regarding withdrawal treatment, their perceptions of what they 'needed' may have been affected by feelings about what they 'wanted'. During the interviews, the sample were asked to comment on the treatment they received from GPs and also what they considered personally as the best method to 'come off'. It became clear that the responses given were moulded by a number of factors, for example, the effect of a given drug on the individual concerned and the user's previous experience of other forms of medication. However, particularly where the interviewee was undergoing withdrawal treatment at the time of interview, a further significant factor was the current treatment itself. Obviously, given the nature of addiction and the despair that it can produce, especially after several 'bites at the cherry', interviewees 'needed' to believe that it was 'going to work this time'. Thus, when asked about the 'best regime for coming off', most of this group of interviewees cited their current treatment programme.

With reference to treatment involving the prescribing of other drugs, the majority of respondents expressed concern about the addictive nature of the drugs themselves. This was particularly the case with patients who had been given methadone reduction over a relatively long period of time, say two to three months. As one user explained:

I mean, I've detoxed six times now and I never have any problems coming off smack. Just three or four days' turkey and I'm alright. At least with smack, I know how long I'm going to turkey. With meth you never know. It could be a month, or three months. You just never know.

In those instances where Valium had been prescribed, several interviewees had become addicted and, once off heroin, would have to repeat the weaning process with Valium. This can be just as traumatic and lengthy as coming off an opioid, as the following interviewee experienced:

I was still taking the heroin and now I'm addicted to Valium as well. I've been, y'know, trying to get off them as well, cutting them down. I mean, for six months solid, he was just writing these scripts out for loads of Valium. I said to him: 'Can't you give me methadone or isn't there a Detox Centre I can go to or something?' Well, he said: 'No. Just keep taking these.' He wasn't really interested.

Turning to those who were referred by the GP to another agency, a major problem experienced by this group was the length of time they had to wait for an appointment (see also Watson 1985). This occurred in the following instance:

I went to the doctor, but he just sent a letter to the Detox Unit and I had to wait three months [for the appointment]. I told me mum about it and she said we can't be having that and got on the phone to the doctor, but he wouldn't even come out and he took me off the [practice's] list. After that, it just got worse. I was really bad by the time I got there, y'know what I mean. I was on two bags a day when I went to see me GP and I was on between a quarter and half a gram when I got to the hospital.

Referrals were made to either the local Drug Detoxification Unit or the Regional Drug Dependency Unit. The regimes of both units came under considerable attack from the interviewees. This is perhaps a reflection of the user's perception of treatment as being synonymous with the prescribing of methadone, while the above-mentioned medical units use a psycho-therapeutic approach with drugs such as methadone and Librium playing only a secondary role. The criticisms that users gave can be grouped under four headings.

First, medication. The regime in the Detoxification Unit consisted of five days' methadone reduction followed by two weeks of Clonidine. The interviewees stated that all patients were treated in a similar manner regardless of the size of their habit and that the quantity of methadone and the length of time it was given were inadequate. As one user with a 2-gram-a-day habit noted:

If you drink a good bottle of meth, you get a good hit, like, but up at the hospital, they give you those tiny plastic containers. They started me off on that much [indicates with his thumb and forefinger approximately $\frac{1}{2}$ inch apart]. I thought they were joking with me at first. Honest to God, that's how much they started me off on.

Second, patient status. In general, users were treated on an out-patient basis, living at home in the community and visiting the clinic at intervals. There were beds available for those with particular problems, such as those who had been injecting over a long period. However, both units limited the number of in-patients to two at any given time. Given that treatment lasts from two to three weeks, a maximum of 100 users can be treated on an in-patient basis per annum. The main criticism levelled here was that users found it difficult to come off while still living in an environment 'full of junkies'.

Third, side effects of medication. This criticism was levelled at the Detoxification Unit where Clonidine formed part of the regime. Clonidine is generally used to treat raised blood pressure and also migraine, but is also used to lessen the effects of withdrawal. Users reported instances of dizziness, nausea and the swelling of joints. In many cases, particularly where the interviewee had previously undergone this form of treatment, they simply threw the Clonidine away.

Fourth, back-up facilities. Users generally complained that, once treatment was over, they were left to their own devices in the community. In the main, this situation was created by, firstly, the distance between the units, especially the Regional Unit, and the communities in which the users live; and, secondly, the lack of available staff with, for example, the local unit having the equivalent of two full-time staff to cover home visits over the whole area.

Demand for the services offered by these units has varied considerably with a consequence that the length of time between first contact with the GP and first appointment has fluctuated between two weeks and three months. The length of waiting lists is affected by a number of factors. On the one hand, variations in the supply of heroin resulting from police crackdowns on dealers or occasional droughts may result in the short-term increase of take-up of detoxification facilities as users try to 'top up' the shortfall in street supplies. However, a further significant factor has been the change in the way that users themselves view these units. In effect, 'word got round' the user networks that these regimes were a 'joke' which resulted in a noticeable drop in the referral rate. So much so, that the local unit, which had previously only accepted referrals from GPs, sent out letters to a variety of agencies, such as the probation service and the social services, asking for referrals from them. This 'lack of confidence' stemmed primarily from the prescribing practices of the units combined with a general 'fear of turkey' amongst the user group, as the following interviewee explained:

> No, I never went there [to the Detoxification Unit]. I haven't heard too highly of it, like. I don't know whether it's true or not, but I don't think they give you much medication and whatever, when you go down there. They don't let you cut down gradual. You've got to stew it out almost right away.

As noted earlier, in addition to treating patients themselves or referring them on to another agency, GPs had a third option, that of effectively doing nothing. Practically all the interviewees had experienced this at some time during their drug career. It must be pointed out that some interviewees stated that they 'abused' their GPs, for example, 'hitting' their GP for methadone when there was a 'drought' of heroin. Some users become quite 'professional' at this, as was the case with the following interviewee:

You get into psychology. You learn how to handle the fella. You'd go in and see him and he's sitting down, so I'd stay stood up, so I'm above him and that gives me a psychological advantage straight away, doesn't it? And I'd be aggressive and loud, but not aggressive towards him, but be loud and strolling up and down, making out I was a damn sight worse off than I was and all that. Storming up and down the place saying just give me one last script, you can't cut me dead and can't you give me something and I'll cut down on this last one and all this. And I'd say I was down the docks last night trying to rob the life-rafts, getting the first aid kits and trying to get the Omnopon and all that, and I nearly got caught, can't you help us out? Then he'd say OK and give us some.

However, there were many instances cited where GPs felt that they could not 'help' users even when this was the first time that they had sought it. The following quote records the experience of one young couple:

I had murder with [my GP] 'cos, when I went, I was in a bad way and me mam took me up the doctor's and he just said: 'I won't give you methadone. How much are you smoking?' and I said 'About a gram' and he said: 'Well, all I can advise you is to go out and buy a gram of heroin and just wean yourself off.' Me husband had the same trouble with other doctors and he went to two. One said he didn't want him on the books, he just didn't want to know. And, when we moved, he went to another and he said: 'You've got no chance. You got yourself into it, you can get yourself out of it.' But the one I eventually went to was very good.

In addition, these user histories point to the fact that the receptionists of some surgeries were instructed to turn away 'addicts' or, at least, segregate them from the rest of the patients. In these instances, users were sometimes forced to resort to subterfuge to gain access to their family doctor. In the following case, the interviewee tried several GPs before using this tactic:

The receptionist would say: 'What's wrong with you?' and I'd say: 'Well, actually it's a bit personal and I'd sooner see the doctor about it,' and they'd say: 'Oh, we can't let you see the doctor until you tell us what's wrong with you.' So I'd say: 'Alright, I'm a heroin addict.' This is about five or six receptionists I said it to and they said: 'Oh, no. The doctor doesn't deal with them. You can't see him,' or 'The books are full', y'know. So anyway I found this doctor and said to the receptionist: 'I've had a bad back. I just want a clearance note off a doctor just to say that I'm fit for work.' Right, so she agrees, says: 'O.K., you can see the doctor.' So I went into the doctor's surgery and I said to him, I said: 'Look, I apologise. I got into your office under false pretences, but there was no other way. I wouldn't have been able to see you.' And I told him what me problem was and what he ended up doing was, he put me on six Valium a day, which did no help whatsoever, y'know what I mean.

An additional problem for those on methadone arose when they tried to 'cash in' their prescriptions. In the first place, many pharmacies do not dispense methadone. Secondly, those that do put up barriers to segregate the 'junkie' from other customers. This occurred at the main dispensing chemist in Wirral's largest township:

The one in town's got a big sign up in the window now saying as from the 1st April, we will only do methadone prescriptions in between two and five o'clock in the afternoon, right. So, if you're in to see your doctor at five at night and get a script, you've got to wait until two the next day.

Finally, there were the three informants who had come to terms with their heroin use, wanted to stay on it, but were sick of the 'hassle' and lack of maintenance facilities. After several attempts at getting maintenance in Wirral, one user continued to obtain supplies of street heroin, financed by working and occasional dealing. The second went to the Liverpool Drug Dependency Clinic which gives maintenance, but did not accept Wirral residents. He lied about his address and so received methadone on a maintenance basis. The third moved further afield, along the coast to Southport where the Drug Dependency Clinic also prescribes methadone on a maintenance basis. He is living with his girlfriend, who is also a user, in a seedy hotel on the sea-front which, according to the manager, is 'full of junkies on social security'.

These user experiences will tie up with a process we describe in Chapter 9 concerned with the changing relationship between medicine and the heroin user seeking treatment. In particular, the refusal by GPs to treat heroin users and the deep disagreements between psychiatrists about how to respond to users will be highlighted. However, treatment is only part of the complex process of coming off. Of equal importance are those social factors which come into play when the user or former user is back on the streets.

And after the treatment?

On completion of detoxification and frequently during it, the user has to come to terms with two further related problems: the psychological and social aspects of dependence. In the following quote, a young married woman with two children describes the urge to use following detoxification. In this particular case, the interviewee had been admitted to hospital with hepatitis and pancreatitis and given a methadone reduction course whilst recovering from the operation:

It makes me cringe when I think how stupid I was. I came out [of hospital] on the Good Friday. I didn't have any children to come home to. They'd been taken care of. I came out on the Good Friday and, on the Saturday morning, stitches still in and everything, I got up and thought to myself: 'I'm going to have a smoke'. And I got [my husband's] stuff and started smoking it. Well, I was putting it on the foil and I thought: 'This could kill me', but it was that strong the urge to have it, I didn't care.

Although the availability of heroin on Wirral's housing estates has varied considerably, supplies are at most a short rail or bus journey away. Thus, there is always the problem of temptation, as the following former user pointed out:

Since I've been on this course, I've been on the bus a few times. I've seen this fella on the back of the bus with his bird and that and I walked down and was sitting by them and he was tooting gear, y'know, behind the back seat like that and he threw a load of gear over to me and said: 'Here, d'you want some of this?', y'know, monging, off his head, like. And I went down to this bird's down by the library two weeks ago and this same fella came in with a gram and he was like that, giving out big smokes. I've been in this position loads of times, like.

Obviously, under such circumstances the former user is in need of all the support he or she can get. The attitude of immediate family and friends is crucial. Family support, however, can have unintended effects, as was the case with the following interviewee:

My dad caught me injecting in the bedroom. He didn't catch me with heroin actually, he caught me injecting coke, but I was on heroin at the time. It was a shock to them, but they stood by me. They've done more than they should've really. They made it too easy for me. I think that's why I was on it for so long. Y'know, I always had a home to go to. I always had three meals a day and cigarettes and things bought for me.

It is especially difficult to keep off when both partners in a relationship use heroin. Most of the women and one of the males mentioned this problem. One young woman stated that it was impossible for her to come off and stay off while her partner was still using:

The thing is, he has been using for such a long time. I can't see him coming off ever. He's only twenty and he's had six detoxes already. He's going in for another one next month, but I doubt if that will work either. I only accepted this [methadone] maintenance course to make sure he went on one, too, because if I hadn't, he would have carried on using gear and I couldn't have handled that.

The following young informant describes the importance of the three principal supports in his life since his release from prison: his family, his girlfriend and cannabis:

I've got no mates 'cos they're all on smack. I can't hang around with anyone, if I hang around with anyone that's a smackhead for more than a couple of days, then it's going to be tempting, so I've got to keep meself

away from them. Me family have been great, y'know. I mean, after all
the shit I gave them they've really stood by me and me girlfriend as well. I
don't even go out on the street now unless she comes with me. I usually
sit in and watch telly or play sounds until she comes round and then we
go out together. She's never used so, if anybody tries to hassle me, she
just fucks them off, like. Another thing is the pot, like. I've got to have
something to fall back on. I haven't got to smoke pot, but I do and I think
that's more security than anything, knowing that you've got a bit of pot
which you can put down and you can say: 'Oh, I don't want none of that
today, I'm not in the mood for it.' The next day, you could say the same
and then, a couple of days later, you'll build yourself a joint. If you talk
to most ex-smackheads, they all fall back on something. If it's not
alcohol, it's pot and drink's worse in my eyes because you can become an
alcoholic. You can't become a potaholic.

The supportive role of other drugs was mentioned by a number of the
sample. The user does not only have to overcome the physical aspect of
dependency, manifest in withdrawal symptoms, but also psychological
dependence. Part of this dependence is simply being used to being 'under the
influence' or 'stoned' for a long period of time and drugs such as cannabis and
amphetamines may go some way to overcoming this problem. However,
several respondents mentioned their dependence on the ritual aspect of their
heroin use. This form of dependence has been well documented for injectors.
An example of this was given by one of the sample group who said that he had
a recurring dream, or nightmare, which climaxed 'the moment the pink of the
Diconal mixed with the red of the blood in the syringe'. A similar phenomenon
was noted by two of the 'chasers', one of whom stated:

Just getting over the chasing was part of it. I started doing it with pot,
breaking a little bit, squashing it on the foil and smoking it as though I
was having a chase. I know it sounds stupid, but it, like, made me feel
better than if I just smoked a joint with it.

These twin problems of psychological dependence and social pressure were
regarded by the majority of users as more difficult to overcome than the
physical aspect of their addiction. Several stated that this was why they would
not go to a GP or a Detoxification Unit, even as an out-patient. The logic of
their argument was that, if they are not able to detoxify *in situ* then they will
never come off. For these, the 'solution' was self-medication in the street
environment. One interviewee 'detoxed' nine times, six times with various GPs
and three times in local and regional Detoxification Units. The longest he had
ever stayed off was six months, at the first attempt. Subsequent periods of
'staying clean' never lasted longer than one month. At the time of interview, he
had cut his habit down from 2 grams to 0.25 gram a day and was 'saving up'
small amounts of methadone that he'd bought in doses of 50ml at £5 a time:

I've been doing a lot of that lately. Been getting hold of a bit of meth, but
it's fairly hard to come by at the moment. There doesn't seem to be much

of it about, not even many DFs, so I've been trying to stock up lately. The ideal is for me to stop out here on me own because, if I go into a unit or something and stop, it's quite easy to go straight back on the gear. Whereas, if I stopped out here in me own environment, I think I'd have more of an argument to stay off it because I'd have worked hard to stop.

Given the general distrust of authority amongst the user population and the problems encountered in obtaining treatment and successfully coming off in the community, there is obviously a need for a service which is seen by users to be impartial. Such a service could act not only as a mediator between users and official agencies, but also deal with those aspects of heroin use that these agencies are unable or unwilling to resolve. In terms of Wirral, this function is carried out by the local Drugs Council which provides a 'drop-in' service for users and their families, a 24-hour telephone service, two-week induction courses with follow-up counselling, and residential facilities for those who need to 'come off the street'.

The 61 individuals in the sample can by divided into three distinct groups. First, there were those 18 individuals who never had any contact with the Drugs Council. The reasons that they gave for this varied considerably. Six stated that they were embarrassed to talk about their habit 'in public'. As one user remarked:

I don't like the idea of getting up in front of everyone and saying: 'I'm a junkie. Look at me.' It's degrading. I mean, we're human beings as well, you know.

Another five thought that talking about it was a waste of time. In the words of one young male:

They only bullshit you. It's pointless going round to places like the Drugs Council to talk about it. The last thing that you want when you're turkeying is to talk about gear. You just want to forget it.

Of the remaining seven, three were imprisoned before they could contact the Council, two were afraid that they might be recognised walking into the Council's offices, one had a 'habit so big' that he thought it would be a waste of time, and one had never heard of the service.

A further 29 initially went to the Drugs Council because of some external pressure: in 15 cases the GP had stipulated counselling as a complement to medication; five had court cases pending and thought that attendance at the Drugs Council would mean a lesser sentence; five were pressurised by family members to seek counselling; and four were advised to attend by their probation officer or social worker.

In only 14 cases did the user 'volunteer' in the first instance to go to the Drugs Council. Again, motivation varied from individual to individual. Six had problems with the medical profession: two wanted maintenance and couldn't get it, the other four came to the Council to ask for advice on changing their GP. In the remaining eight cases, four arrived out of curiosity after friends had received counselling, two were pregnant and afraid to tell their GP, and two wanted help on release from prison.

The interviewees' subjective evaluations of the service provided by the Drugs Council are intimately related to the reason why they went there in the first place. Obviously 'successful' counselling needs a minimum commitment from the user, and amongst those who were 'forced' to go there was a general consensus that counselling was a waste of time. The majority only attended sessions on one occasion. As one young male noted:

> I had better things to do than just sit in an office talking. It's like my probation officer, you just get bored talking to them. It's the same old questions when you walk in there. A bit like being at school.

The exceptions in this group were a number of, generally older, users who had been required to attend by their GP. To a certain extent, age was an important factor in that the older user was more likely to have reached the stage in his or her career where all the other options had been tried at least once. Similarly, most of the 'volunteers' were older and, in the main, contacted the Drugs Council because of problems with other agencies. The consensus, here, was that the Drugs Council provided a worthwhile service. On the one hand, they stated that, because they felt relatively isolated from the 'rest of the world', counselling sessions provided a means of release, particularly as they felt that the counsellors were more in contact with their own reality than individuals from 'official' agencies:

> When I came off, I felt I needed to sort of keep in touch, sort of speaking to people that know what's going on and know what's going on in ex-users' heads, y'know. It helps sort of talking to people that know the score and that. Y'know, instead of trying to explain it to people all the time. I think talking to them helped me a lot to get over those first few months.

On the other hand, they felt that counsellors were generally helpful in sorting out their most pressing needs, particularly in finding them a more sympathetic GP and resolving their accommodation and financial problems. However, while the resolution of the immediate crises in the user's life and the provision of a counselling service to help users think objectively about their position may provide the 'ideal conditions' for coming off, users must still come to terms with their addiction, their lifestyle and whether the alternatives on offer hold sufficient promise.

Summary

The interviewees whose drugs careers have informed this chapter sought help either in the form of counselling or medical treatment. This decision, as will become increasingly clear when we discuss the 'hidden sector', makes them a minority group amongst users. Certainly, at any particular time during the research period, the majority of users were not in contact with either counselling or medical agencies. Furthermore, even with this sample we have noted that many were either pressured to present for help or ambivalent about the helping regimes. And, finally, according to their own motivational accounts it is more often the lifestyle and the hassle of being dependent on a drug which is illegal, expensive and difficult to obtain which users regard as 'the problem' rather than heroin itself. There is, then, considerable evidence in this chapter to support the view, held by many deviancy theorists, that legal sanction, prohibition and societal reaction are as important in the aetiology of a drug career as any primary causes such as personality.

We must also take note of the variety of heroin career patterns amongst the 61 respondents. Clearly the diversity of their experiences and needs and the significance of age and gender in defining the trajectory of drugs careers must be matched by flexible counselling and treatment. Monolithic detoxification regimes, when viewed from the patient's perspective, appear what they really are — insensitive and inflexible.

Finally, we must recognise the contradiction which 'problem' heroin users and a reactive society face. On the one hand, it seems that it is the illegality and stigma attached to heroin use which cause users their problems more than the drug itself. On the other, there is no likelihood of this socio-legal context becoming more liberal in the immediate future, and so the 'hassle', the dangerous lifestyle, the broken hearts and broken homes, which users and their relations suffer from, will continue. In this sense heroin is a real problem. Moreover, it is a 'spectre' which hangs over a predominantly deprived urban 'underclass' of unqualified, unskilled and unemployed young adults. It is for this stratum of users and their families that heroin is the dragon with a sting in its tail, not the hidden middle-class users who can afford their habit and avoid the police and courts. Such contradictions are not new in the sociological literature. Nevertheless, the damage which heroin use has done to working-class families is very much at odds with '1970s' British literature. The latter, with its emphasis on drug use as victimless, and youthful deviance as relatively harmless and a form of generational and gender-based continuity in working-class families, is clearly in need of revision.

Note

1   There is much work to be done in explaining heroin use by women in terms of their gender roles (see Dorn and South 1983–4).

5

Moving down user networks

Following on from the analysis of known heroin use, the second stage of the ethnographic work involved contacting the 'hidden' sector, those who had used heroin during the course of the prevalence study period, but who had not come into contact with any of the ten statutory or voluntary agencies surveyed. This stage, then, took our research a step further in that it penetrated the submerged section of the 'iceberg' and offered some insight into this large and hidden sector of users. Given the 'action' orientation of our research project, the analysis of unknown heroin use centred on two specific tasks: assessing the size of the hidden sector and, thus, reaching an overall estimate of the number of heroin users, to enable the Borough of Wirral to forecast future demands on its services; and identifying variations in the drug career patterns of users in the hidden sector as compared to those of known users, in particular the specific reasons for the lack of contact with agencies.

The achievement of these aims imposed certain restrictions on the methods used during this stage of the field research. On the one hand, the sampling process had to generate as many categories of user as possible and so account for the variations found in the known sample relating to age, sex, class, township, and so on. Failure to do this would have created serious problems for both the generation of a reliable multiplier factor and comparability between the two samples. On the other hand, this goal, that is, a sample sufficiently large so as to make it representative, had to be weighed against time, staffing and other factors which imposed a practical limit on the size of the sample. As Glaser and Strauss (1967, p. 52) point out, sampling procedures involve a set of complex decisions concerning time (the overall period of contact and the frequency of contact within that period); space (the geographical location of contact and the social context of it); and person (the selection of the individuals themselves). Sampling procedures, then, necessarily involve a series of compromises.

A network approach

It is impossible to see, hear and participate in everything that is happening in a given social environment. This problem is exacerbated when dealing with an illegal activity such as heroin use, especially when some form of sampling is necessary. Moreover, 'unknown' heroin use does not lend itself to the more usual sampling procedures such as random sampling, saturation sampling and dense sampling. Given the need for an extensive approach within the limitations noted above, and given that the first stage of the fieldwork demonstrated that heroin users generally confine themselves to specific networks, it was decided to use a 'network analysis' approach using the technique of snowball sampling, or chain referral (Fraser and Hawkins 1984, p. 82). This would enable us to map out the informal social structure of the 'heroin community' in a variety of geographical locations.

We chose four townships as sites for the network studies. The initial prevalence survey identified a high correlation between unemployment and other social deprivation factors and also revealed that 75 per cent of heroin users were aged between 16 and 24. Therefore, unemployment and opioid use amongst the young were chosen as the two factors by which to rank Wirral's 48 townships. After ranking, townships were classified as having very low, low, medium, high or very high levels of unemployment and opioid use amongst the young. Four townships (A, B, C and D) were then selected as being representative of the various combinations of these factors shown by the 48 townships as a whole (see Table 5.1). Township A stood apart from the rest, having both a very high level of unemployment and a large number of known opioid users. This township was treated as a special case. The other three townships were chosen as characteristic of the majority of the rest of the townships in the borough. No townships which demonstrated 'very low' opioid use were included in the snowball samples as these were invariably small villages in largely rural settings. They had small populations and few, if any, known opioid users and so their exclusion did not significantly alter the findings presented below.

Having chosen the four townships that were to be the location of the snowball samples, it remained to select the zero stage of the samples, one individual from each township with whom to start the referral chains. Each of

Table 5.1 Profile of townships

Township	Unemployment			Known heroin use amongst population aged 16–24		
	Type	%	Rank*	Type	%	Rank*
A	Very high	33	1	Very high	8.6	1
B	High	25	4	High	6.2	2
C	Medium	9	24	Medium	0.9	26
D	Low	8	27	Low	0.4	33

*Rank out of 48.

these users had to meet certain criteria. First, they needed to have already been contacted and interviewed during the study of the known sector. Personal details obtained here provided the foundation from which to make the selection. Second, they should have been using heroin regularly for a period of at least two years. This would ensure that they would be firmly established within heroin user networks and not peripheral to them. Third, and most important for the success of the networking, concerned the establishment of personal rapport between fieldworker and informant. As Whyte (1943, p. 300) noted in his classic study of Chicago street gangs, acceptance by informants depends much more on the development of personal relationships than on any explanation concerning the reasons for conducting the research.

The establishment of personal relationships was not as crucial during the study of the known sector where informants had been randomly sampled. Their participation hinged on a variety of factors such as personal situation at the time of receiving the response sheet; feelings of obligation towards the two agencies involved in the sampling; perception that being interviewed might help them in the future; boredom with prison life; and simple curiosity. As the study of the known sector progressed, it became increasingly difficult to generate further interviews as most of those amenable to interview had already sent in positive response sheets. It was at this stage of the process that the perception of the fieldworker as 'alright' became important. Given the density of heroin-using networks, word spread quickly that a research programme was being undertaken and later informants frequently mentioned that the fieldworker had previously interviewed someone known to them. Several of these later informants from the known sector stated that they had only decided to agree to participate after a close friend or acquaintance had been interviewed.

For successful snowballing, though, being seen as 'alright' is crucial from the outset and the earlier work in the known sector played an important role in this. A further contributory factor was that the fieldworker came from the region and had an accent and working-class background similar to those of many of the interviewees themselves. Building upon this, the fieldworker targeted known users in a number of townships as possible participants in the zero stage of the later snowballing process. These were contacted regularly on an informal basis for several months between their initial interview as part of the known sector sample and the start of the snowballing phase. They were selected on the basis of their general knowledge of the drug scene (several were dealers and thus the centre of specific networks) and their ability to communicate that knowledge. The danger of using 'encyclopedic informants' has been well documented. As Henige (1982) points out, there has been a tendency to use such informants to the exclusion of others, with the result that data are biased towards the experience of a small number of individuals. During the course of the fieldwork under discussion here, they were used principally as a means of access to user groups and also as foils for cross-checking general data provided by other informants.

During the process of interviewing the known sector, it was found that, because of the enigmatic lifestyle of heroin users, an average of three or four home visits were necessary before the interview with any given individual successfully took place. Thus, it was decided to limit the referral chain for each township to 15 individuals, a total of 60 including the zero stage. Given this numerical limit and the need to interview users as far removed from the known sector as practicable, it was also decided to restrict the number of referrals from each informant in the chain to two. Thus, excluding the initial informant, each snowball chain would encompass a minimum of three further stages (see Figure 5.1).

Having outlined the snowballing process itself, the following sections will present the findings concerning the two principal tasks that it sought to accomplish — measuring the size of the hidden heroin sector and identifying variations between the profiles of known and unknown users.

Assessing the extent of the 'hidden' sector

While data relating to the known user population are important, they cannot alone define the extent of total heroin use in a given community (see Chapter 3). On the one hand, data such as notifications by GPs to the Home Office, police arrests for heroin offences, referrals to Detoxification Units, and so on, not only reflect upward and downward trends in heroin use itself, but also external factors such as changes in official policy and availability of street heroin. On the other hand, once estimated, the known user total still

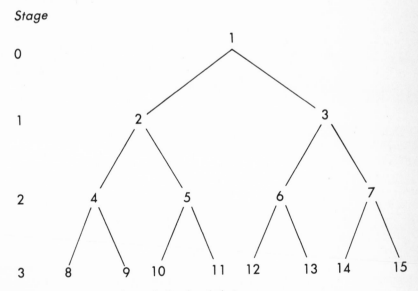

Figure 5.1   Structure of snowball referral chain

represents only a proportion of the total user population and, thus, a multiplier factor is needed, that is to say, a ratio of unknown to known heroin use, in order to determine the size of the total heroin user population (Hartnoll *et al.* 1985a). In this section, we present a number of methods for producing a multiplier factor. It will be demonstrated that, because of the great variation across Wirral, several such factors are needed to obtain an accurate estimate.

Method 1: Using snowball nominees only

The first method is relatively simple and consists of comparing the number of known to unknown users amongst individuals in the snowball sampling frame itself. As noted, a total of 64 individuals who had used heroin during the prevalence study period were contacted and interviewed. Four of these were members of the networks under observation, but lived in neighbouring townships and so were excluded from the quantitative analysis which concerned itself with the known–unknown ratio in specific townships. Each of the remaining 60, 15 from each township, were asked whether they had been in contact with any of our list of ten agencies during the same prevalence study period. As a cross-check, they were also asked to give their initials and date of birth which, together with their sex, provided an identity code. This was then compared with the known user list for each township. In six instances, all male, the informant did not wish to provide his date of birth, although year of birth was given. The relatively small numbers involved in the known sector meant that initials, sex and year of birth were sufficient to effect a reliable double-counting procedure. The results of this process are given in Table 5.2.

It will be seen, first, that there is clear variation in the ratios between the townships; and, second, that the ratio of unknown to known use is much smaller for the two working-class estates (A and B) than the two middle-class townships (C and D). The principal problem with this method, however, lies in the small size of the sample group, only 15 users being interviewed in each township. Even one extra user in a group would cause a substantial change in the known–unknown ratio. Clearly, then, this method is subject to considerable error.

Table 5.2 Estimate of the extent of the hidden sector: Method 1

Township	Unknown users	Known users	Ratio unknown : known
A	8	7	1.1:1
B	10	5	2:1
C	11	4	2.8:1
D	12	3	4:1

Method 2: Nominee peer group

The 60 interviewees were then asked to state how many of their 'five closest friends' (of the same sex and living in the same township) regularly used heroin during the year in question. They were also asked how many of those identified had sought medical treatment, counselling, or had been arrested for drug offences during that same period. It is clear that data obtained from these questions relied heavily on hearsay rather than on the actual knowledge of others, as well as of the informant. In addition, because informants rarely knew the actual date of birth of their friends, it was not possible to obtain an accurate identity code. However, as with Method 1, initials, sex and year of birth provided a 'next best' identity code. In all, a total of 170 identity codes were generated using this method.

Table 5.3   Estimating the extent of the hidden sector: Method 2

Township	Number of friends using	Number known	Ratio hidden : known
A	49	25	1:1
B	44	14	2.1:1
C	40	9	3.4:1
D	37	7	4.3:1

The results of Method 2 show remarkable similarity to those obtained by Method 1, even though almost four times as many individuals were encompassed by the nomination process. Again, there were considerable variations between the townships, the greatest distinctions being between the working-class and middle-class communities. What is interesting, however, is that the ranking of ratios is the same as that obtained using Method 1. This was in fact found to be the case with all four methods discussed here.

Method 3: capture–recapture

The figures generated by the snowball sample itself and by the nominations of this sample group have given us two sets of ratios of the hidden to known sectors. We will now compare these to those produced using the methods of Hartnoll *et al.* state that the two samples must be independent. That is, each 'indicator–dilution' technique. In short, this involves the use of two samples of the same user population. These are compared and the results used to assess the extent of the total user population (N) according to the formula $N = N_1 \times N_2 / X$, where N_1 is the number of users identified by first sample, N_2 is the number of users identified by second sample, and X is the number of users in N_2 previously identified by N_1.

Hartnoll *et al.* state that the two samples must be independent. That is, each of the samples should be a random representative sample of the whole user population in a specific geographical location and in a given time period. Thus, it would not be advisable, for example, to compare a sample of heroin users generated from GPs' records with one produced from the files of a local Drugs Council, because some GPs require patients to attend counselling sessions to complement medical treatment, so that patients who have seen their GP about their heroin use may be more likely to occur in a sample generated by a local Drugs Council than users who have not sought treatment from their GP. In addition, the time spans of N_1 and N_2 must, first, be identical, if a comparison is to be made, and, second, must be of sufficient length to produce a valid result (see Hartnoll et al. 1985a).

Thus, for each of the four townships, it should be possible to compare the users identified by the first prevalence study with the users generated by the snowball sample in the same township to produce the required ratio of hidden to known use. With reference to the networks under study, the samples cannot be considered random as such, because it is not true that all users in the township during the prevalence period had an equal chance of being selected. Nor was the sample 'systematic', in that, for example, every fifth house in every street in the township was sampled for users. Rather, it was a 'haphazard' sample in that users who arrived to 'score' at the houses under study while the researcher was present were asked to participate and ask their friends to participate. Thus, those who had already 'come off' were underrepresented in the sample. However, this raises the question of whether the ratios produced are underestimates rather than the question of the independence of the two samples.

Using the Hartnoll et al. formula, and substituting for N_1 the total of unique (initials/date of birth/sex) identity codes generated by the first prevalence study for each of the four townships, for N_2 the 15 individuals nominated for each township during the snowball sampling (that is, excluding the zero stage), and for X the number of identity codes occurring in both samples, we arrive at a total user population of 814 for these townships during the prevalence period. Given that 237 of these were 'known', this gives a ratio of 2.4:1 of hidden to known users for the four townships as a whole. The figures for individual townships are given in Table 5.4. The ratios generated by the capture–recapture method display a remarkable similarity and identical ranking to those obtained by the first two methods.

Table 5.4 Estimating the extent of the hidden sector: Method 3

Township	N_1	N_2	X	N	$(N-N_1)/N_1$
A	93	15	7	199	1.1:1
B	125	15	5	375	2:1
C	12	15	4	45	2.8:1
D	7	15	3	35	4:1

Method 4: triangulation

Hartnoll et al. also describe a second method of assessing the size of the total user population and, thus, a means of finding the ratio of hidden to known users. This is the analysis of anonymous networks by 'triangulation'. Here, users already contacted are asked to provide a description of other users in their network. The details of each individual nominated are compared with those of other nominees to see if they match. If an individual is nominated by at least two others, then this is taken as confirmation of this individual's existence in the network.

Users contacted through the snowball sampling procedure were asked to provide the initials and sex of up to ten persons in their township who they knew to have used heroin regularly during the first prevalence period. A number of interviewees (12 per cent) stated that they did not object to nominating others for the actual snowball sample itself because they could first ask the nominee, but would not furnish identity codes on an indiscriminate basis. The other 53 nominated a total of 297 other persons. Female informants were more likely to provide identity codes and to provide more of them than males. Any nominated initials/sex identity codes which occurred more than once were treated as the same person. This resulted in a total of 163 unique individuals who were all nominated by at least two other persons amongst the snowball group. These identity codes were matched against those generated by the prevalence study. A total of 66 were identified as known users and 97 as hidden. Figures for each township network are given in Table 5.5.

The ratios obtained by triangulation are somewhat smaller than those produced by Methods 1–3. However, it is possible that the ratio of hidden to known use provided by Method 4 is nearer to the true ratio than the others because, although it involved less accurate determination of identity codes, the larger numbers of nominees involved may dilute the effect of extreme cases. Nevertheless, it must be also stated that the ratios are probably still underestimates because identity codes did not include date of birth and, thus, the double counting procedure may have eliminated persons who should have been included.

Table 5.5   Estimating the extent of the hidden sector: Method 4

Township Type	Total nominated	Total unique	Number hidden	Number known	Ratio hidden:known
A	109	64	27	37	0.7:1
B	83	43	28	15	1.9:1
C	49	27	20	7	2.9:1
D	56	29	22	7	3.1:1

Producing an overall ratio

The four methods, then, have provided four separate sets of ratios of unknown to known heroin use for four different townships. These are listed in Table 5.6. However, we cannot use a simple average (mean) of the four ratios for each township to produce a single multiplier factor because they were determined by different methods. Similarly, the range is not broad enough to produce a median ratio. Therefore, the modal ratios of each township type, that is, those which appeared most consistently, were used as multiplier factors (see Table 5.7).

Table 5.6   Estimating the extent of the hidden sector: the four methods compared

Township	Method 1 Ratio	Method 2 Ratio	Method 3 Ratio	Method 4 Ratio
A	1.1:1	1:1	1.1:1	0.7:1
B	2:1	2.1:1	2:1	1.9:1
C	2.8:1	3.4:1	2.8:1	2.9:1
D	4:1	4.3:1	4:1	3.1:1

Table 5.7   Estimated overall prevalence using modal ratios

| | Township | | | |
	A	B	C	D
Unemployment Rate	33%	15%–28%	9%–14%	1%–8%
Unknown/Known Ratio	1.1:1	2:1	2.8:1	4:1
Known Opioid Users	98	601	191	242
Unknown Opioid Users	108	1,202	535	968
Sub-Total	206	1,803	726	1,210

Total = 3,945

As Table 5.7 shows, when these modal ratios are projected over Wirral's 48 townships, we reach a total figure of 3,945 heroin users in the borough during the prevalence study period. However, given that in our earlier prevalence study the township of residence of 173 users was not known, and assuming an intermediate ratio of 3:1 for these users, we can calculate that there are an additional 692 users.

This gives an overall prevalence total of 4,637. However, it should be remembered that this figure will be an underestimate in the sense that it excludes occasional users — 'chippers' and 'dabblers'.

Profile of snowball interviewees

In Chapter 4, we pointed out that the profile of the known sample group was skewed away from the 'typical' young unemployed heroin chaser identified by the prevalence study because of the very nature of being a 'known' user in treatment. To a certain extent this bias is rectified in the snowball samples as those interviewed were in various stages of involvement in heroin use and thus show a greater degree of variation in terms of both their social and heroin career profiles.

Social characteristics

The informants contacted during the snowball sampling procedure were aged between 18 and 32 at the time of interview. They were on average 18 months younger than known users, 22.5 years as compared with 24, with 56 per cent being 22 years old or under compared to 47 per cent for known users. The age difference between the two groups, however, was not evenly distributed: males in the hidden sector were on average only 10 months younger than males in the known sector, while females were 2 years 8 months younger. As noted in Chapter 4, women are more likely to become known at a later stage in their heroin career than males for a number of reasons. On the one hand, if they are mothers they are more likely to delay seeking help from their GP for fear that their children will be taken into care. On the other hand, they are less likely to be apprehended or detained by the police for drug and/or non-drug offences.

The two samples displayed similar profiles in terms of sex, although the snowball user group had slightly more females. The majority of the 'unknown' males were single (74 per cent against 65 per cent) and less women were married (19 per cent against 28 per cent). However, more women were cohabiting (38 per cent against 6 per cent). In part, this tendency towards cohabiting can be explained by the fact that the known users were randomly sampled, whereas the hidden sector was sampled through nomination and interviewees' partners formed a prominent part of the sampling frame.

Only six (9 per cent) of the network sample were employed at the time of interview while 58 (91 per cent) were unemployed. Thirty-six of the unemployed (62 per cent) had never worked since leaving school, while the rest had had at least one job during that time, but had subsequently become unemployed. The modal length of unemployment at time of interview was three years, slightly less than that of the known sector. This difference is accounted for by the younger average age of the snowball sample. Of those who had previously worked, the reasons given for their current unemployed state were as follows: short-term MSC contract, or redundancy, 36 per cent; dismissal because of lateness, etc., due to heroin use, 23 per cent; imprisonment, 14 per cent; collapse of business, 9 per cent; pregnancy, 9 per cent; boredom with job, 9 per cent. The employment profile of this group parallels that of the known sector but emphasises the fact that most had never worked or had only had a 'work experience' employment rather than lost their job because of heroin use.

Drug career characteristics

All the snowball interviewees were initiated into heroin use during the current outbreak, with 71 per cent first using heroin from 1982 onwards. At this period of time, heroin supplies were much more regularly available and user networks were already well established. Thus, it is not surprising that, even though the snowball group were older than their known counterparts when they began using drugs for recreational purposes (a modal age of 16 against 15), they were initiated into heroin use at an earlier age (a modal age of 16 against 17). Experimentation with heroin for interviewees in the hidden sector, then, began at a much earlier stage, after an average of six months of recreational drug use instead of 17 months.

Given this shorter period of experimentation with other drugs prior to heroin use, it could be expected that these informants would have exhibited less variety in their pre-heroin polydrug use. This was not the case. Users sampled through networking showed a similar polydrug profile to those in the known sector, with two important exceptions. First, far fewer of the snowball sample had used other opioids prior to heroin use (13 per cent against 23 per cent), and this was restricted in the main to older males (modal age of 29). This was probably due to the restricted street availability of opioids such as Diconal after 1982, the very period during which the majority of the younger interviewees were initiated into heroin use. Second, heroin was the first drug used for recreational purposes by 20 per cent of the snowball sample compared with only 8 per cent of known users. This can be attributed to a number of factors: the increased availability of street heroin in Wirral during the early 1980s; the periodic droughts of pot and speed at around about the same time (some of the users suggested a direct relation between these phenomena); the existence of large numbers of users initiated in the 1978–81 period who acted both as models to emulate and who were also probably the first dealers the new initiates came into contact with.

The heroin initiation patterns of this sample are quite similar to those displayed by the known sample with the exception of younger females. On the one hand, the average number of females' friends who also used heroin was greater, at 2.8 out of 5 against 1.8 out of 5 in the known sample. The figure for males remained constant at 4.2, probably because it had already reached 'saturation' point. On the other hand, and directly related to the latter, whereas in the known sector females were three times more likely to have been introduced to heroin by their partner rather than a friend, amongst the snowball females, just as many females were introduced by a friend as by a partner. This change in female initiation patterns is also reflected in the reasons they gave for experimentation with heroin in the first place. Curiosity and partner's use both fell dramatically from 44 and 50 per cent to 19 and 38 per cent respectively, whilst 'peer-group pressure' rose from 0 per cent in the known sector females to 24 per cent amongst the snowball sample females. This finding warns us against concluding that women get into heroin and sustain regular use solely because of male associations and partnerships.

Having mapped out the general social and drug career characteristics of users interviewed in the four snowball samples, the following section will discuss why these users had not come into contact with the various voluntary and statutory bodies expected to deal with the 'heroin problem'.

Staying hidden

The vast majority (82 per cent) of the snowball group were using heroin daily during the prevalence study period, compared with 61 per cent of the 'known respondents', yet only one-third became clients of the relevant agencies during the same period. In addition, even though more of their 'five best friends' were regular users of heroin, fewer of these were 'known' to agencies, an average of 24 per cent against 40 per cent. Even 12 months later, after the second

Table 5.8   Known users in snowball sample

| | Townships | | | | |
	A	B	C	D	Total
Not known	5	7	11	10	33
Known to first prevalence study	7	5	4	3	19
Known to second prevalence study	3	3	0	2	8
Total	15	15	15	15	60
Total known*(%)	67	53	27	33	45

*To both prevalence studies.

prevalence study, more than half of the snowball group were still 'unknown' to the various agencies surveyed (see Table 5.8).

Several factors contributed to the low proportion of these users known to Wirral's 'care' and 'control' agencies. The first concerns the structure of the snowball sample itself in which the 60 interviewees were evenly distributed between four 'representative' townships, 15 from each. However, according to our first prevalence study, it was those areas characterised by the greatest levels of social deprivation that contained both the largest absolute numbers of users and the highest proportions of users. The snowball sample, then, by giving them equal weighting, overrepresents users living in areas with less social deprivation. Thus, the proportion of known users in the community as a whole is likely to be greater than that given in Table 5.8.

Second, almost three-quarters of these interviewees had been using heroin for two years or less by the start of the prevalence study period. As Chapter 4 noted, the average time lag between daily use and first contact with an agency was 2.6 years. Thus, the majority of this group had not reached the point of their heroin career where becoming known is most likely and so were less likely to show up in crime statistics, medical records, and so on, than longer-term users.

Third, the sample contains a relatively high proportion of females (33 per cent). An earlier study (Parker et al. 1986a) demonstrates that male users are more likely to be known than female users, especially to legal agencies such as the police and the probation service. This is corroborated by the data obtained from the snowball sample which show that, while 38 per cent of males were known, only 20 per cent of females were known. Thus, given that more males are likely to be known than females and that males are underrepresented in the sample, this too suggests that Table 5.8 underestimates the level of known users in the user population as a whole.

Fourth, contact with agencies varied considerably between the four townships. Table 5.8 demonstrates that a greater proportion of users known to both prevalence studies came from the two townships with higher levels of social deprivation. In part, this is due to the higher profile of socio-legal agencies on working-class housing estates where the user is more visible. In addition, middle-class families are more likely to have access to off-Wirral treatment for their children, particularly in the private health sector.

The fifth concerns the development of close-knit user networks in Wirral in the late 1970s and early 1980s, just prior to the 'initiation' of the majority of the snowball sample. This facilitated the regular distribution of heroin along specific channels readily identifiable by users and so 'scoring' moved off the street and became a less hazardous occupation. Consequently, it is possible that these new users were less likely to be caught by the police. Given the profile of polydrug use noted in Chapter 4, these networks also facilitated the street commercialisation of other drugs. Of particular importance, here, was the increased availability of methadone and DF118s, both of which are used as heroin substitutes in time of drought. So users could avoid contacting their GP during such times of crisis because these drugs were easily obtainable.

Similarly, for those users contemplating 'coming off' or cutting down their drug use the links between members of township networks and those between the networks themselves provided a dynamic body of 'knowledge' based on the user's direct experience of available services. Clearly, fact and fiction become intermingled in such a process, but, as Chapter 4 points out, the idea that 'treatment equals methadone' developed at this time in Wirral, as did native knowledge concerning which agency or GP did or did not prescribe methadone. These combined to produce a situation where users unable to obtain prescribed drugs began to develop other strategies for 'coming off' such as the purchase of street methadone mentioned above.

The final factor concerns the idea that 'being known' should be avoided at all costs. Obviously, because the possession of heroin is illegal, users must maintain a low profile for fear of legal sanctions. Rightly or wrongly, many users assume that there are close connections between all forms of authority. To these users, a visit to the doctor may eventually mean a visit from the police. Compounding this, there is also considerable confusion amongst the heroin-using population as to the actual nature of the 'registration' and 'notification' of addicts. The two terms are used interchangeably and viewed with some awe, especially by younger users. Thus, many users prefer to stay hidden regardless of the problems that this might cause their families or themselves. An example of this was given in Chapter 4, concerning female users with children who did not seek help from their GP because they assumed a direct link between the GP and social services. It is only at times of real crisis, when these individuals have reached the end of their tether, that they will break this code and make themselves known. The consequences of this gulf between 'hidden' users and official agencies will be more fully explored in Chapter 9.

Summary

Using four different methods, this chapter has demonstrated that the 'hidden' sector represents the greater part of Wirral's heroin-using population, some two-thirds of the total.

Despite important differences between the hidden and known sectors in relation to gender and class, there is in most other respects a remarkable similarity. However, given that users in the hidden sector are slightly younger, and have not been using heroin for as long as the known users, it does seem highly likely that many more of these 'hidden' users will surface, either because of prosecution, pregnancy, physical illness or their own decision to seek help of some sort. In Chapter 9 we suggest that the provision of user-friendly, confidential services will encourage this surfacing, whereas repressive policies, stigmatisation or persecution will discourage it.

6

Living with heroin: four case studies

To illustrate the analysis of earlier chapters, we present four case studies selected from the 125 interviews with known and hidden heroin users. These are not 'ideal types'. They do not represent four predefined, distinct categories of user. Rather, these mini-biographies have been chosen because between them they cover the gamut of the life experiences of the user group as a whole. They show not only the 'stages' through which a user may pass, but also the range of strategies open to the user at any given time, and they illustrate the social processes that determined the trajectory of the pattern of heroin use in each case.

The presentation of these case studies in the form of 'life stories' is intended to give the reader more of a 'feel' for what it is like to be a heroin user. However, life stories are not simply recollections of past events as they occurred. The process of narration involves an *interpretation* of these past events in light of other events that have been experienced since. As Bertaux-Wiame (1979, p. 29) notes, the act of telling one's life story is an encounter with reality. While this encounter seems to be limited to an account of the past, it is in fact very much determined by the present. On the one hand, it reconstructs the past from the present point of view. On the other, and more importantly for us here, it gives meaning to the past in order to give meaning to the present.

In these life stories, then, each user is providing an interpretation of past actions which is intimately linked to his or her present-day existence. However, in the social context of heroin use in a given community, it is just as important to understand how events are perceived by the participants as to know that they actually happened.

The names given to each narrator are, of course, fictitious. Due to lack of space, it was obviously not possible here to provide complete transcriptions of each interview, including the interviewer's questions. Occasional additions have been made to the text to aid understanding; these have been kept to a minimum.

Alan

Alan is 35. He has been injecting heroin since he was 16 years old. He and his girlfriend, who has used heroin for six years, live in their own home in one of Wirral's well-heeled townships. Until his recent financial problems, which stem from his heroin use, Alan was a self-employed builder. For the main part, he has financed his habit throughout by working, although he does admit to dealing occasionally when work was scarce. He has never engaged in acquisitive crime such as burglary, because this would contradict his 1960s 'peace and love' philosophy. He has sought treatment on a number of occasions and has come to the conclusion that he cannot break the habit and that what he needs and wants is a maintenance regime, preferably on heroin — something that the medical profession in Wirral does not want to give him.

> Opiates! I don't know if I like the word smack. It conjures up the bad image about opiates on a general scale, y'know. Well opiates, I began to dabble with them when I was about 16, after experimenting with cannabis, amphetamines, LSD, opium, and moving in a circle ... I was probably what you'd say was a hippy at the time, y'know ... The Isle of Wight rock festivals. Both of them ... And unfortunately I'd eaten a large quantity of this Afghani black and I was really bombed out and I slept half way through Jimi Hendrix and I could have kicked myself. Anyway it was make love not war and that kind of thing seemed to go along with it, y'know. I smoked pot and a pipe of peace and things like that and everybody was tripping out and all the rest of it and that's how initially I got into it. They were first introduced to me when I was 14 by friends who were 16, 17, 18, who at that time were going to Art College and they introduced me as it was then to five-bob deals of black and stuff like that, y'know. So I got into it through those channels ... I was very open-minded towards drugs then and I would try anything that was going provided that I didn't think it was too dangerous ... and I did like to analyse the thing, the substances, through literature. I wouldn't take anything that I thought might be too harmful and detrimental to my health, y'know. And opium and opiate derivatives just came along with it, y'know. But I wasn't into heroin on a full scale for a few years after that. I tried opium, and my first experience with anything really hard, using it intravenously, was when I used Omnopon which was from a lifeboat, y'know, from the life-saving equipment on a lifeboat. I'd come across that and used that intravenously and thought well I really enjoy this and at the time the people who I knew were breaking into chemists and things, they used to come across very powerful substances, diamorphine, crystallised cocaine, morphine, that whole range of opiates

and also amphetamines, black bombers and all the rest of it and then opium became more available on the streets and it was round about the same price as cannabis was at the time ... We're talking about 1970, 69–70, and I decided that I liked this kind of ... I was more inclined to enjoy this type of drug as opposed to amphetamines, y'know, which at the time left you feeling a bit uncomfortable the next day. I'm being polite because of the recording. But I used to enjoy speed quite a lot, y'know, but never, I never used it intravenously. I always used it on the tongue or used dexies and black bombers, y'know, swallowed pills and things. And cocaine when it was available, but it was very rare at that time, y'know, but opium seemed to be very stable, there was always opium available and that was the thing that I would always try to achieve, to obtain, y'know.

I was living at my folks and then my parents found what they thought was a lump of cannabis in my pocket. What it turned out to be was a lump of clay that I'd moulded into what looked like a piece of black and wrapped up in silver paper just fooling about and they really freaked out and they kicked me out and had the police involved and everything. They analysed it and found that it was mud, a piece of clay, y'know, but them not being all-forgiving, they suspected that I was using drugs, y'know, so they kicked me out of home and I went to live with my grandmother and then I had more freedom there to do as I pleased and hence started going to pop festivals and things and enjoying them and getting off on them and mixing with that whole subculture if you like. Oz magazines. The whole thing, the whole spectrum that went with it, y'know, as you know yourself, if you were around in those days and going to concerts and one thing and another. And that was the beginning of my drug history. And then I had tried harder and harder to obtain opiates and would do my damnedest to get hold of morphine, opium, diamorph and anything, y'know ... It is good to be able to talk to somebody who has experienced the whole spectrum of drugs because then they know what the hell you're talking about, y'know. It is important. I mean, a lot of social workers, they try to understand and they are sympathetic, but they just haven't got a clue, y'know. They've just got no idea what it's like. Withdrawal symptoms and all this kind of thing. Difficulty of obtaining substances, trying to find the cash to buy the stuff, y'know, all the things that go with it, social problems, domestic problems, mental health problems. Although, fortunately up to now, I never seem to have had many health problems with using opiates. You lose a lot of friends, though, when you're on opiates. The image they've got is different from other drugs. They're frightened through ignorance I think more than, y'know, me personally. And when I've attempted to stop using in the past, I've had the feeling, the feeling has definitely been positive, where your friends do tend to come back to you and say: 'Oh you're looking well. How're you getting on? Come and see us for a pint, I'll meet you in so and so and we'll go for a pint', and all that, y'know. They do come round again, but once they find out you're using again, they just drop you like a brick ...

I'm working on my own house at the moment. The thing is, it's a vicious circle, it's Catch 22 really, 'cos I used to have a good self-employed business, going painting and decorating and I used to have a good clientele and that and I found over the years that, when it became harder and harder to score and the prices rocketed and all that, it got out of hand, out of proportion, that I was spending more and more time off the job than I was on the job, looking round to get the stuff and I found I was unable to carry on working without the drug, because I just felt so bad and I couldn't climb ladders and I thought I was a danger to myself and anybody else that I had working with me, y'know. And I'm saying to Mrs Jones, yeah I'll do whatever, y'know, I used to have some good contacts with Estate Agents and that and they would just ring me up and say will you come and do so and so and we want it done within six or seven days, y'know, a house that they were selling, that they'd want completely doing from top to bottom inside and out. Well at one time, I was able to cope with that, but eventually I found myself taking three and four weeks to do it, y'know, with time wasting for going out trying to score and stuff like this, just to feel as though I could cope with the job. And it became difficult, so in the end, rather than committing myself when people phoned up saying can you come and do a job for me, rather than do it badly and not being there and being unreliable I'd say: 'No. I can't do it.' Although I was capable of doing the work and doing a good job, I didn't want to be letting people down and that. Now I've lost all my contacts and I'm unemployed at the moment, y'know.

I'm working on my own house at the moment and I'm waiting for a grant off the Housing. I've got an overdraft at the bank to finance it and I find myself using this cash, y'know, to buy gear. That's no good at all, because when that goes the job stops and I don't get paid off the grants people and the bank holds the deeds and, if I don't forthcome with the grant money, then I will lose the house. I've already lost one house and a business and a car, two cars, and all the rest of it. I've gone bankrupt once through it and I can see the same thing happening again ... I've spent, I don't like to think about it, y'know, hundreds and thousands of pounds, I've spent. It's a sin really and I can't handle it. I realise that it's not only an illness, I suppose, but it's quite selfish in a way. I've got this thing that I like, that I like to do, but maybe it's selfish, but on the other hand, I don't know. There's a conflict there and people get, well people like a drink or a smoke or whatever they do, they get off on whatever they do, but it's just damn not as expensive as the habit I've got, y'know ...

The longest period I've abstained was two-and-a-half months. I just found it really hard, y'know. Nigh impossible. I mean, I was using a couple of grams a day, so I was still feeling bad withdrawal effects even after that two-month period. During the 70s, I was using more or less steady throughout. When it was available. It wasn't always available like it is now. It was pharmaceutical as well, so there was no problem of having all this muck mixed in with it like there is now. But, in 1984, I had one of these crash courses of methadone, 14 days, which was just a piss in the can. It was absolutely useless. It was no good for me. Fifty mls on the first day and then 40, 30, 20, 10. Reducing by probably 10 mls a day which is just useless. Well it was useless compared to the amount I'd been using, y'know. Forty mls of methadone is probably equivalent to what? Half a gram or something like that. It's pathetic. Well everyone gets the same thing. Everybody is categorised in the same mode, y'know. If you're a junkie this is what we give you, y'know. And this is what you get. A 14-day crash course and that's the end of it and when that's finished away you go ... Then I was in the hospital for a fortnight and they gave me Librium and I was really ill at that time. They didn't give me methadone, they just gave me I think it was 30 milligrams of Librium and two sleepers of a night time ... I tried, like, I did try, but it was just no good. I didn't feel as if I was gonna succeed at all. I stayed there for the duration to try and prove to myself that I was able to do it. Stick it out for the fortnight, I couldn't take any more and the day I got out, I went and scored. I just couldn't handle it any more.

I would like a maintenance methadone course, y'know, if possible. Ideally, to be honest I would like a diamorphine maintenance course, but I don't know if that's possible these days to pick up a prescription once or twice a week and be able to do it that way instead of having the hassle of having to go on the street. You see, I'd like a family. I'm trying to get a home together. I'm in the middle of a government grant on my house and by the time I get that together and spending money, which I shouldn't be doing, on junk, y'know, and I want to start a family and that, y'know, and try and be respectable, but it just doesn't seem to be available under this health service, this National Health Service, although I do know people who have it prescribed. I think it is a bit unfair, y'know. Because they're a year younger than I am, two years younger and they've been registered now for six, seven, eight, or nine years. But I think the political climate on that changed a few years ago, when there was the big influx of heroin onto the market ... It's just this problem you might say that I've got, y'know. Although I know it's a problem in the eyes of the public and the Health Service, I try not to think of it as a problem personally, y'know what I mean.

I'd like to be able to overcome that feeling that it was a problem to everybody else. It's got a bad stigma to it and that's what's the main problem with it, y'know, this junkie in a dirty squat with a needle hanging out of his arm and OD'ing and dealing on his doorstep and everything and looking like the pictures you see of people falling to bits, but for me personally it's not like that, y'know, I do try to conduct a normal law-abiding life. I mean, especially at my age, I don't wanna be running round the streets doing all this monkey business and getting into trouble with the police and all that, y'know. I'm just too old for that

now. I don't wanna have to be confronted with that situation much
longer and I feel that I've got to do something, y'know ... But I do feel
isolated, yeah. Like the people that I mix with, they have the same kind
of feelings. They can't look people in the eye and say: 'Oh yeah, I use
heroin. So what!' Because they get strange looks, etc., etc. They're not
accepted wholly in society and I feel that why the hell shouldn't they,
y'know. It's all the stigma attached to it and all the things that people
have to do to obtain it. Robbery and muggings. Which I'm trying to
avoid not to do. I could no more go out and mug an old lady than I don't
know what ...

Bill

Bill is 23. He is single and lives with his mother in one of the older council
estates. He began using heroin at the age of 18 and has used it more or less
regularly for five years. Since leaving school, he has been employed as a
draughtsman and this is his only source of finance for his habit. This has
created severe financial problems and at one time he was heavily in debt to the
bank. He has attempted to come off on several occasions and at the time of
interview was undergoing methadone withdrawal and has been heroin-free for
two months.

It just took over from the lack of draw on the estate. It just sorta took
over from that. I was at a stage where I was used to getting something
like cannabis or whatever and with none a that being round I thought a
bita this won't do me any harm and it just took off from there ... I'd been
living away and when I first come back into the area a few of me friends
was into it. One mate had been into it for a while 'cos he used to go away
to sea. At that time there was no pot around, it was all heroin, really. I'd
tried it once or twice before, a coupla times when I was younger, but I
wasn't over keen on it because of the, y'know, just 'cos of the name it'd
got really, y'know, having to inject it and that. Then, I think with just
being able to chase it and whatever, it didn't seem as heavy as injecting it.
So that's how I really gorr into it ... It was just being with mates really.
There was a lorr of it going on at the time, y'know. There was no way
really that you could've avoided coming into contact with it anyway at
my age on the estate. I think everyone would've come into contact with it
and I think it was just up to your own individual self really whether you
took it or not.
    I tried other opiates, but I 'aven't used them now for years. I tried when
I was about 18, 19. I tried some Palfium once or twice an' some
morphine, that was it really. I never gorr into them, and then it was just
all heroin on the estate ... For the first few months I was just having it
now and again and then I was having a bit more. It took about nine
months before it started getting a grip of us really. And then I was using it
more or less daily for years ... It hasn't really worried me, though. It

doesn't worry me now at the moment. It's just the dependence really, y'know. All the time you waste.

It takes a lorr a time scoring and that, y'know. You've got no time for anything else. It just takes up all your life, really. With me workin', by the time you got home from work at 5 o'clock, it might take you till 9 o'clock at night to score some nights. You're sorta runnin' about all the time, so you don't get time for anythin' else really. It just starts getting you down eventually ... I'd buy grams whenever I could as it'd save me going over to Liverpool to score. I've bought all sorts really, but normally in the first week or two of getting paid, I'd buy a gram or whatever and make it last for four or five days, so I'd sort of have a quarter a day out of it. Before the clampdown, I used to be able to score round here, there was that many places that you can score really. It was rife with it, really, so there was no problem with scoring. Now you have to go to Liverpool and rather than go over each day and gerr a quarter, I'd rather buy a gram and keep hold of it. I did use more at first when I was buying grams, say a year ago, when I was doin' that, but, say this last year I was trying to pace meself out 'cos I knew that I'd run outa money eventually, so I had to try and make it last ... I could handle working while I was using. In fact, I couldn't have worked without having a chase before I went in and during the lunch hour. Then I'd have a good blast when I got home, like. I did notice I was slipping a bit. I wasn't concentrating as much as what I could do, but I got over it really ... How much I used really depended on what time of the month it was, on when I got paid, like. At certain times of the month and whatever, I could be using half a gram a day and towards the end of the month whatever money I had left went on it.

I did get into debt at one stage, but with actually working you can get your hands on anything really. A lorr a money, really. If you're with a bank and you've been with them a few years, they'll give you all kinda loans. At one stage I owed about 1,500 quid. Well it isn't a lot, really, but I suppose it is when you're on the gear 'cos you never get round to paying it off. It took me a long while to pay it off. I had to eventually sort it out after a few sorta threats off the bank. So I eventually gorr it out the way, but I wouldn't like to gerr into that position again.

That was round the time when I first went to see me doctor. About a year an' a 'alf back and the methadone course was over ten days and really it was no use whatsoever. By the time I got to the end of the course, I was still picking up the pieces. I hadn't really sorted anything out socially or whatever and so I just got back into it. Straight back into the routine just after a coupla weeks. There was just so much around. I just couldn't avoid it, really. Like now it's quiet this side of the water, on the Wirral, very quiet. So really you can actually avoid not coming into contact with it, but, two years ago, just really everywhere you walked there'd be someone dealing or whatever, so you couldn't really avoid it. I'd only gone say two weeks without it, but it takes a lot longer than that to actually sort yourself out, anyway ... The second time I tried to come off was when I went to stay with me sister and I took her DFs and just stayed in, y'know. I used them, about 14 a day, for a week and I managed to stay off for about a month. But at the time, I suppose I never really wanted to come off. I suppose I got more bullied into it through me family really, to get off it, so I never really had the push to come off it. This time I do feel as though I've gorra stronger urge. I don't know, the last few times I've tried to come off, I haven't really wanted to come off, thinking about it now. I just drifted into it 'cos I was forced into it by me family.

I think that this time I decided meself that I was gonna come off when I got paid. Normally I'd wanna come off when I'd run outa money and I'd got nothing else to do 'cos I've never gone robbin' or anythin' like that. I'm sick of it, really, just sick to death with it. It's just built up over the last coupla years really. The last year, I've cut down considerably anyway. I've been using, but not as much as I was, say, two or three years ago. I had to pay off what I owed the bank. Anyway, I've cut down considerably and every now and again I'd try an' stop and fall off the rails again. It's dragging on, it's been dragging on for a year, but I'm getting there slowly and I feel a lot more confident than last time. I decided to go up and see me doctor 'cos at the time I 'ad about £600 that I could've got me 'ands on. Well, I'd just been paid, so there was no problems about me having money to score, so I think I'd just set me mind that I wanted to sort meself out once and for good. He's giving me a three-month methadone course, to bring me down gradual ... I'm going to the Drugs Council as well though. But even that's difficult 'cos I have to travel to get there after work. But that helps just to talk to someone who knows what your going through, but, when all's said and done, I think it's down to yourself, really. No matter how many people you see, I think it's all down to yourself in the end.

Carol

Carol is 28. She lives with her two children, aged seven and five, in a terraced council house in suburbia. She has no legal income other than state benefits. The father of her children is presently serving a two-year custodial sentence for burglary. Prior to his imprisonment, his burgling and dealing activities financed their heroin use. After several brushes with the law, which included a term of imprisonment for supplying heroin and the temporary taking into care of her children, she began to shoplift as she felt that she was less likely to receive another custodial sentence if she was caught.

It was me feller really. He was into it and I just tagged along, like. I'd used dikes, DFs and things like that before, so I knew what I was getting into. He didn't want me to try it, 'cos he knew that I'd like it. I don't know whether it was because he realised how hard it'd be for us to get

enough for both of us, or whether he knew he was off his head and
needed someone around who wasn't, y'know what I mean, to look after
the kids and sort things out, like.

I was using regular for about two years after that until I was sent
down. John was burgling and dealing at the same time, so we had a
regular supply, like. John had done a burglary and bought a quarter ounce
and started selling it out in bags. Then we had a bit of hassle off the
bizzies. They couldn't prove nothing, but they warned us that they were
onto us and, if they heard we was still dealing, they'd be round like a
shot, like. So John said that's it, we're gonna have to knock the bags [on]
the head and just give out grams, like, and he had two lads working for
him doing the bags ... The way it worked was they'd give him 70 quid for
a gram and they'd sell it in fiver or tenner bags. He'd get a quarter ounce
a day, sell five grams and keep two grams for us, like. And we'd make a
hundred quid as well ... So that was going alright for a while. Y'know,
with only these two lads coming round the house and then both of them
got bust in one of the lads' house and they blew me up as the one who
was supplying them. So the bizzies come round here and bust me for
possession. I got bail for that 'cos of the kids, like. A couple of weeks
later, they bust the house again. They must have had the house under
surveillance, like. So anyway, they found a quarter gram upstairs and
wanted to do both of us for it. Then this woman plod who was with me
upstairs while I got dressed, 'cos I was in me nightie, said to me: 'Look.
You're up soon for possession and are gonna get sent down anyway. So
why don't you admit supplying and then John can stay out and look after
the kids, like?' So they had a big argument downstairs, this woman plod
and the others and I said to John: 'Look. There's nothing I can do.
They're gonna take me away anyway. So I might as well admit the
supplying as well.'

So that was it. They took me over to Cheapside and I was remanded in
custody. I got 18 months, six of them suspended. They said it was a gram
in court ... About four months after I went down, John was involved in a
car crash. He was driving over to Liverpool to score and had the
youngest lad with him. He hit a lamp-post and fractured Mike's skull.
They let me out for the day and then, when he regained consciousness
five days later, they let me out again to see him. Then John got done for
burglary and he was put away five days before I got out. So we sort of
bypassed each other. The kids had already been put in voluntary care due
to the car crash and I couldn't get them back until three months after I
came out. I was drug-free, like, so they had to give me them back.

Then this lad who'd been padded up with John come round to see us.
He came round when he got out and just stayed, like. Well, he was back
into the gear and started dealing, so there was always plenty around and
I got back into it as well. I suppose it was loneliness really. There's
nothing to do round here. The neighbours don't have nothing to do with
me and I only see me mam once a week or so. Anyway, he got bust and I

was on me own again. So that was me with a habit and two kids to look after on 36 quid a week social ... I started dealing meself then. This guy who lives round the corner had just come out and he'd started up in business again and he was laying it on me a gram at a time and I was doing it out in bags. Things started getting really heavy again after that. The house was like a madhouse. Y'know, people coming round all hours to score and all that. I didn't want people coming round, I'd rather take it round to theirs, but you just couldn't stop them, y'know what I mean. If someone's turkeying, they're not bothered about your position, they only wanna get their hands on some gear, like.

That scared me a bit, so I had to stop dealing. I'd been using most of it anyway, like. I didn't make any bread out of it, just me own gear, like, and I was still in debt to this lad who was laying it on me. I owed him over 200 quid ... I went the doctor's and told him about me back. I must have strained it or something playing with the kids. While I was on the smack, it hadn't bothered me much 'cos smack's a good painkiller. Anyway, he started prescribing me DFs. Fifty a week. So that got me over the turkey. He's been giving me them for eight months now. Y'know, I just get a repeat prescription every week. I don't think he knows what he's giving me 'cos you're just as addicted to them as you are to smack. When I first went, I thought I'd only get them for a couple of weeks at the most. Maybe he's forgotten about me or something.

But I was still broke, like. As I say, I only get 36 off the social and when I get it on a Monday, I usually spend 30 right away on food for the kids. Y'know, so at least they've got their dinners, like. So then I started going shoplifting with me mate 'cos six quid's not gonna get you nothing, is it? I mean, that doesn't even get your fags let alone shoes and that. And the way these two go through shoes is terrible.

At first, I was only going out a coupla days a week. Y'know, we'd get down town early or go over to Liverpool and spend all day out. Between us we'd get about 200 quid's worth of goods, like, jeans, tops, kids' clothes. Y'know, things that you can always get rid of. People always need clothes don't they and they'll always buy them off you if you're selling them at half price ... We'd just sell them round the estate, round the houses, like. No bother ... Then the guy round the corner, y'know, the one who'd laid the gear on me, came round last month and started getting heavy about the money I owed him. Two hundred quid, like. He was going mad. Shouting and threatening me in front of the kids, like. So, he got me handbag and took off with me bottle of DFs and me book from the social and said he'd give it me back once he'd cashed enough to pay the bread off.

So that was me destitute, like. With no money off the social and only me family allowance coming in. So I had to go out shoplifting every day then. That's what I've been doing six days a week for the last four or five weeks. It would've been easier if I got into dealing again, but I can't afford any more heavy scenes with the law. If I go inside on a drugs

charge again, I might as well kiss the kids goodbye, y'know what I mean
... I'm up in court next week on a shoplifting charge, but I'll only get a
suspended or something like that. Me probation officer doesn't know I'm
using again. As far as she's concerned I've been drug-free since I come out
of stir.

It's getting harder and harder, though. Once you've been going to the
same shops a lot, y'know, just standing around and not buying anything,
they get to know you. I mean, I'm a pretty good shoplifter, like, but
yesterday all I got was two bloody Barbie Dolls, y'know, a tenner each,
like. Everytime I got near anything a floor walker'd be on me like a shot
... I'm frightened though. I'm frightened of the probation and the social
services finding out that I'm using again, 'cos when I came out this time,
they said to me that, if I ever went back on the smack, that the kids'd be
took off me, no two ways about it ... But what can I do? I'm destitute,
like. I haven't even got social at the moment. At least with that you've got
food in the house, if nothing else ... I just can't see it ending at all and I
don't know what'll happen when John gets out. He gets out in eight
months. I just hope he stays off the gear and we can get straightened out.

Dave

Dave is 19. He lives with his parents and sister in a big terraced house in one of
the older townships in Wirral. He began experimenting with drugs when he
was 13. At 15, he started to dabble with heroin and within 12 months he was
using it daily. He began to finance his habit through burglary. After much soul
searching, he decided that the only way he was going to come off was to be
totally separated from the drug scene. On his arrest for burglary, he admitted
to all his previous offences with the sole aim of obtaining a custodial sentence.
At the time of interview, he had been heroin-free for over 18 months.

I started taking smack at school, 'cos everyone in the —— estate at that
time was taking it and that was the only place you could buy pot and I
sent one of me mates out from school one day to buy some speed and he
come back with smack and said this is all I could get and I said I don't
want none of that, but in the end we ended up doing it because we was
bored and we had nothing else to do. We was dabbling for about a year
then ... Well, it began with just when I got me money each week, 'cos I
had a job, a weekend job with me uncle and I'd get me money and I'd just
go out and score, get a coupla bags or something and then me mates'd
come round here and say, 'Can I do a smoke in here?', y'know, and so
they would and they'd give me a smoke for coming in here and eventually
it started getting, like, from weeks, from weekends to days, becoming
every day, like.

It just took off like a rocket from there. Every night. All the time ... I
started off by smoking it, but later when I was injectin' it, I found I got
more of a hit, y'know what I mean. It lasted longer and that, a.better hit.

So, in the end, I was mixing it with cocaine. So I was doin' about a gram of heroin, a gram of cocaine, the most I ever done was a gram. I was mixing the two and injecting the two, which was pretty weird and I think the only reason I was mixing the coke in with it was 'cos it was cheaper at the time ... Because there was a bit of a drought on and it filled in, like, for the smack ... I started getting into a heavy scene though, y'know, building up a debt, like. There was some people round here that were selling gear that weren't smack'eads and they'd do you a lay on without any rings or surety or nothing and you'd say, well, 'Lay us on half a gram and I'll sell it, like', and they'd say, 'Alright', and then you'd go back a coupla days later and say, 'Look. I haven't got the money, yet. Lay me on another half a gram' ... and they'd go, 'Alright' ... in the end, you'd owe them a coupla grams and you'd have to go shoplifting in Chester or something 'cos you couldn't go round town in case they were there ... I didn't really deal much, I couldn't. I'd just end up using it all. However much I had, I'd do it in, like.

I started to take things from the house as well, y'know, little things that I thought wouldn't be noticed. But me mam got suspicious. When I eventually told her, she was devastated ... an' me dad too. They didn't know what was going on, like, didn't know what to do, whether to lock me in me room, or let me out and do what I wanted to do, but in the end, like, I just didn't come back here for a coupla months. I just stayed out, kipping at me mate's and that.

I tried to come off a few times, y'know, off me own bat, like, but there was too much of it around. Everywhere you went, you'd meet a mate who had some gear. I was off for a week which is alright, but during that week I was heavily doped on downers. I was dropping DFs and Mogadon all the time and drinking, just drinking me head off of a night and I wasn't sleeping. I don't think I slept right through that whole week. I'd be in a club till 2 o'clock in the morning and then come home, sit down and be bored until the morning started and then I'd be walking round, taking the dog for a walk in the park. It was horrible, really horrible ... I went to me doctor as well, but if I go to that doctor with a swollen ankle or somethin', she gives me antibiotics, if it's me back, it's antibiotics, if it's a cold, antibiotics. She gives me antibiotics for my heroin addiction. She didn't know what she was doing I don't think. This was before all this publicity, like, but she still should have been sussed out. Then she did get me an appointment with this new clinic that was opening at the hospital, but it was too late. On the day of me appointment when I was meant to go, I got stuck away, went inside ... I'd been going out burgling, like. I'd never done anything like that before. It wouldn't have entered me head, y'know what I mean. But when I was strung out, I'd have done almost anything ... If I'd had no gear the night before, I wouldn't go to bed all night. When I went out robbing, it'd be the early hours of the morning, one or two in the morning, so nobody'd notice me missing here. Just walk down the road here to all them shops and just knock one of them off, bring the stuff back, stash it till the morning and then go and sell it to buy some gear … And I did that about 30 or 40 times, going through each individual shop in a row. I used to go out just on me own, like. Once I'd broken into this solicitor's and all there was there was this big safe, y'know the type I mean, a big square box that was on this big slab of polished wood. Anyway, I thought I'll have this away and I slid it off the shelf and it dropped like a ton of bricks on me leg and broke me ankle. Just then the bizzies came and all the sirens started going in the street. There must have been an alarm in the office, like. So, there's me, in agony with me ankle, hobbling over to the hole that I'd made in the wall of the office. I crawled out into the alley and it was one of those blind alleys, y'know, blocked off at one end, so I had no way out. I just hid in the corner until the bizzies had gone. How they didn't see me, I'll never know, 'cos I was just huddled up in the corner of the alley. Anyway, after they'd gone, I just hobbled round to me mates and stayed there for a few weeks. I didn't wanna go the hospital 'cos they'd have wanted to know how I did it and I would have had to turkey in there. So me mates just kept giving me gear until me ankle got better. That was about three weeks in bed, having a toot to kill the pain.

It's still got a twist in it now, but it's alright, like. I only ever burgled shops. I did go out with one of me mates once and he was going burgling and I needed to do one 'cos I had no money or nothing, strung out, and he went to the Old Hall Estate and broke into a house and I got in through the window with him and I just looked around and saw all these photographs of, y'know like, the family that lived there with the kids and that and I just got this horrible feeling, so I just got out the window and walked away, even though I was strung out and I didn't pick nothing up, I just left him to it 'cos, like, though all the burglaries I'd done, they'd all been shops. I'd never done an 'ouse before.

After that, things started to go downhill. It was getting out of hand, like. I could see meself doing it for years, like. I mean the doctor was no help and I'd been waiting for over a coupla months to get into the Clinic for a detox. So anyway, before I heard that I'd got an appointment at the Clinic, I got caught for one burglary and so I told them about the rest, 'cos I wanted to get off it an' I knew that was the only way of getting off it and I thought, now I've been caught, I might as well get meself stuck down for a bit, like, rather than get a big fine which I wouldn'a been able to handle at that time … So they put me in a detention centre for six months. I come off, like, but they didn't give you no treatment or anything. It did the trick, like. I haven't had any gear for nearly two years.

7

Counting the cost of financing the habit

An exceptional rise in crime

The rate of recorded crime in England and Wales, in 1985, was 73 per 1,000 population, a 40 per cent increase on 1979. Within the Merseyside region, with its much higher rate of 102 recorded crimes per 1,000 population, and a 50 per cent increase over the 1979 rate, lies the Borough of Wirral. But while Wirral itself had a recorded rate of 85 crimes per 1,000 population in 1985, below the average for Merseyside as a whole, this figure represents an 84 per cent increase over 1979. This disproportionate acceleration continued in 1986, as Table 7.1 shows, with Wirral's crime rate growing far faster than anywhere else. Since 1979 it has increased at twice the rate of any other part of the region. Hence, during the same period in which the heroin 'epidemic' has developed, the community's crime rate has soared. In this chapter, we explore the possible relationship between the two phenomena.

Table 7.1 Crimes recorded in Metropolitan Districts of Merseyside, 1979–86 (per 1,000 population)

	Liverpool		Wirral		Sefton		Knowsley		St Helens	
1979	99		46		55		65		46	
1980	106	(8.2)	48	(4.6)	58	(5.5)	70	(7.7)	48	(4.4)
1981	124	(26.5)	60	(30.4)	66	(2.0)	80	(23.1)	58	(26.1)
1982	130	(32.7)	70	(52.2)	69	(25.5)	91	(40.0)	63	(37.0)
1983	127	(29.6)	78	(69.9)	67	(21.8)	88	(35.4)	60	(30.4)
1984	143	(45.9)	87	(89.1)	71	(29.1)	90	(38.5)	63	(37.0)
1985	146	(47.5)	85	(84.4)	75	(36.4)	92	(41.5)	64	(39.1)
1986	155	(46.2)	98	(113.0)	78	(41.8)	99	(52.3)	69	(50.0)

Percentage increase on 1979 rate in parentheses.
Source: Chief Constable's reports for Merseyside Police.

Table 7.2 offers some interesting clues. It shows that, whilst crimes such as violence and the taking of cars have risen in line with national trends, the most dramatic increases have been in acquisitive crimes like the burglary of homes and theft from cars. This rise is quite disproportionate compared to national trends. The 262 per cent increase on the base line for burglaries noted in Table 7.2 for example, contrasts starkly with a regional rise of 124 per cent and a national rise of about 90 per cent. This is certainly consistent with the hypothesis that acquisitive crimes are being committed by drug users targeting their activities to obtain cash or easily resaleable goods such as car radios, video recorders, clothes and consumable goods. However, we must be cautious in making this link, because other explanations are possible. Indeed, the debate about the relationship between heroin use and crime is complex and unresolved. Undoubtedly there is strong evidence that many heroin users were criminally active before ever using heroin (Greenburg and Adler 1974; Gandossy et al. 1980). To this must be added that heroin use and crime may be related to independent factors such as personal, social and economic 'predeterminates' which encourage both types of deviance to occur (see Elliott et al. 1983; Fry 1985). Moreover, we must be wary of considering heroin use in isolation from other forms of drug use (Hammersley and Morrison 1987). It may well be that in some circumstances heroin becomes the drug which both the public and even users themselves 'blame' for crime when in reality the cause is rather different.

What can be said at the outset is that Wirral has not experienced any atypical demographic or socio-economic conditions; nor suffered from social disturbances or public disorders which might have pushed up the crime rate in such a specific way.

In this chapter we investigate the nature of the relationship between heroin use and crime from two quite different but complementary angles. First, we turn to official indicators and try to establish whether drug users are being atypically convicted of acquisitive crime. Hence we report on an investigation based on court and criminal records and our master register of known heroin users. Second, we explore the sources of financing a heroin habit based on self-report data gleaned from 61 of our in-depth interviews with users. Given that neither of these approaches, in isolation, is totally reliable, we would require them to be consistent with and supportive of each other before reaching any firm conclusions.

Court appearances, criminal records and heroin use

The investigation

The first way we approached our search for a relationship was quantitative in nature, being based on police and court records. The research methods were fairly complex and are described elsewhere (Parker and Newcombe 1987). Basically, we took the initials, date of birth, sex and township of residence of a sample of young adults (born between 1950 and 1970) in the Borough of

Table 7.2 Categories of crime recorded by the police, for Wirral, 1979–86

	Burglary of dwelling	General theft and handling, etc.	Theft from motor vehicle	Burglary of various premises	Theft/taking of motor vehicles	Criminal damage and arson	Violence (excluding murder)	Other	Total recorded crime
1979	2,824	4,684	1,553	2,052	2,338	1,065	599	578	15,693
1980	2,919	4,784	1,809	2,026	2,383	1,197	622	657	16,397
% increase on 1979	3.4	2.1	16.5	-1.3	1.9	12.4	3.8		4.5
1981	4,432	5,232	2,406	2,863	2,710	1,536	633	618	20,430
% increase on 1979	56.9	11.7	54.9	39.5	15.9	44.2	5.7		20.2
1982	5,619	5,582	2,767	3,436	3,062	1,687	628	817	23,598
% increase on 1979	99.0	19.2	78.2	67.4	31.0	58.4	4.8		50.4
1983	7,041	7,165	3,092	3,291	2,513	1,781	612	950	26,445
% increase on 1979	149.3	53.0	99.1	60.4	7.5	67.2	2.2		68.5
1984	8,459	7,009	3,249	3,159	3,137	1,850	683	1,771	29,317
% increase on 1979	199.5	49.6	109.2	53.9	34.2	73.7	14.0		86.8
1985	8,908	6,625	3,030	3,103	3,306	2,049	784	777	28,582
% increase on 1979	215.4	41.4	95.1	51.2	41.4	92.4	30.9		82.1
1986	10,238	6,700*	4,822	4,003	3,193	2,731	796	458*	32,941
% increase on 1979	262.5	43.0	210.5	95.1	36.6	156.4	32.9		109.9

*Owing to a change in recording methods by Merseyside Police these figures are estimates for 1986

Wirral and convicted of serious crimes in Wirral magistrates court and Liverpool Crown Court during the first half of 1985. Thus, we had a confidential identity code for 300 local young offenders extracted from court records and made up of the following groups: 100 persons found guilty of burglary in a dwelling; 100 persons found guilty of general theft of goods (worth over £50); 50 persons found guilty of the unauthorised taking of a motor vehicle; and 50 persons found guilty of criminal damage (valued over £50). We then cross-referenced these 300 'offender' identity codes (282 males, 18 females) with our Prevalence Register containing the identity codes of some 1,800 'problem' drug users in order to see what proportion of offenders of various sorts were also known drug users, particularly opioid users.

Another test we applied concerned looking at whether the type and rate of criminal convictions for those we identified as drug user-offenders showed signs of being affected by their drug use. Were drug user-offenders committing more crime and was it increasingly focused on offences such as burglary and theft, the proceeds of which go to buy street heroin? Were any changes concentrated in the 1982–6 period when the prevalence of heroin use had been at its height? Were there any young people who had never been in trouble prior to their dependent use of drugs? To answer these questions we looked in detail at the criminal histories of our sample. We divided all 300 criminal records into five categories: technical offences such as breaching a court order; Misuse of Drugs Act convictions; offences taken into consideration (TICs); acquisitive convictions; and non-acquisitive convictions. We discounted technical offences and TICs from our study and, as there were very few Misuse of Drugs Act convictions,[1] we based our analysis on the acquisitive–non-acquisitive comparison. The results provided us with the necessary data to look at the effect of heroin use on the criminal careers of young adults in Wirral.

Drug use among the sample of offenders

Table 7.3 shows that 106 of the individuals in our sample of offenders were known drug users, and that the vast majority of these user-offenders (87 per cent) were opioid users (almost invariably heroin users). The highest rate of known heroin use is among those convicted of burglary (50 per cent), followed by theft (30 per cent), compared to those convicted of unlawful taking of a motor vehicle (UTMV) (20 per cent) and criminal damage (4 per cent). Are these rates of known drug use higher than we might expect? This question can be answered in relation to the rate of known opioid use in the general population of Wirral, and the overall rate of known opioid use in our sample of offenders.

First, the 1984–5 prevalence survey found that 1.4 per cent of the 16–34-year-old population of Wirral were identified as 'problem' drug users during this one-year period and 1.2 per cent were opioid users. Since the age of 10 per cent of the drug users identified by this survey was not known, it may be estimated that up to 1.5 per cent of this population are known users, and that up to 1.3 per cent are known opioid users. Table 7.4 shows that, employing the higher (estimated) figure for the general population, the rate of known

Table 7.3 Known drug use among 300 offenders

	Total sample	Known drug users	Known opioid users
Burglary	100	55 (55%)	50 (50%)
Theft	100	33 (33%)	30 (30%)
UTMV	50	13 (26%)	10 (20%)
Criminal Damage	50	5 (10%)	2 (4%)
Total	300	106 (35%)	92 (31%)

Table 7.4 Comparison of observed numbers of known drug users among offenders, with numbers expected on the basis of the general population prevalence of known drug use

	Known drug users		Known opioid users	
	General population	Criminal sample	General population	Criminal sample
Burglary (N = 100)	1.5	55	1.3	50
Theft (N = 100)	1.5	33	1.3	30
UTMV (N = 50)	0.8	13	0.6	10
Criminal Damage (N = 50)	0.8	5	0.6	2
Overall	4.6 (1.5%)	106 (35.3%)	3.8 (1.3%)	92 (30.7%)

opioid use is much higher for our 300 offenders overall (31 per cent), and far higher among the subgroups convicted of burglary, theft and UTMV. In numerical terms, our prevalence survey leads us to expect about four known opioid users in a representative sample of 300 16–34-year-olds, whereas our sample of 300 offenders actually contains 92 users. Similarly, if there is no relationship between crime and drug use, we would expect that only one 'burglar' and one 'thief' would be known opioid users, and that less than one UTMV offender and criminal damage offender would be known opioid users. In sharp contrast, we actually found that half (50) of the 'burglars' were known opioid users as were a third (30) of the 'thieves' and nearly a quarter (10) of the car takers. Indeed, only criminal damage offenders had a rate of known opioid use similar to that in the general population. In short, compared with the prevalence of known opioid use in the general population, there is a much higher rate of known opioid use amongst these offenders (with the exception of those convicted of criminal damage), and by far the highest rate of known use is exhibited by those convicted of burglary.

Second, turning to within-sample comparisons, if there are no differences between the rates of known opioid use among the four types of offender, we would expect the 92 cases to be evenly distributed throughout the four subgroups. Such a distribution would lead us to expect about 31 known opioid drug users each among theft offenders and burglary offenders, and about 15 each amongst the car-taking and criminal damage offenders. However, we found 50 known opioid users among burglars, which is over one-and-a-half times as high as expected. In addition, the number of known opioid users among UTMV offenders (ten) and criminal damage offenders (two) is much lower than we would expect if users were equally distributed. Indeed, the overall differences between offender groups are statistically significant, both for the number of known drug users in each group and the number of known opioid users in each group. Closer examination of this overall significant difference reveals that the main source of the effect is the dissimilarity between the burglary offenders and the criminal damage offenders.[2]

These, then, are fairly dramatic findings (see also Mott 1986). They show that a much higher proportion of drug users (predominantly heroin users) than we would expect are present in the offender sample. There is also a strong tendency for heroin-using offenders to focus their crime on burglaries as opposed to non-acquisitive offences such as criminal damage. However, these results do not tell us about the chronology of the heroin–crime relationship. Have heroin users turned to crime or have criminals turned to heroin? Have young people caught up in an expensive drugs habit had to turn to burglary to finance their dependency or are we instead uncovering the fact that young people with a tendency to be offenders anyway have added heroin use to their repertoire of deviance (Burr 1987)?

The exceptional criminal careers of drug users

Before discussing the impact of heroin use on criminal careers, we first need to consider the characteristics of a 'normal' delinquent or criminal career. Most young people go through a rebellious or anti-social phase during their adolescence (Rutherford 1986). The majority of these settle down in late teens, however, and manage to do so without incurring a criminal record. A minority are officially sanctioned partly because their deviance is more serious or extensive and partly because some young people receive less of the protection and support from school or family which might allow their misdemeanour to be dealt with privately or informally. Most young people are not officially sanctioned, and indeed many of these who are, begin to settle down and keep out of further trouble in their late teens. A report on the progress of a national study of the criminal careers of males born in 1953, 1959 and 1963 (Home Office 1985a) shows that one in three had one or more convictions for a 'standard list' offence before the age of 28. However, the great majority had only one such offence. Given that this national 'cohort' study looks at young males of similar age and committing similar crimes to our Wirral sample, it provides a particularly useful comparison. The most significant finding from our point of view is that, for the 1953 cohort, a mere 5.5 per cent of males 'who had before the age of 28 been convicted of 6 or more offences accounted for 70 per cent of all the convictions of the group to that age' (p.1). Given that by definition our sample of 300, with a mean age of 21, already had more than one conviction, we must consider, given the rate at which they are gathering convictions as young adults, whether they are a potential microcosm of this national '5.5 per cent' group of long-term offenders. Is the Wirral picture dominated by a small group of 'life of crime' young adults who failed to settle

down in late teens and for whom heroin use is merely an additional deviant
feature of their lifestyle?

Two hundred and seventy-nine of the 300 Wirral sample fell into the 17–32
age group with a mean age of just over 20 years. For technical reasons, we
used this group in analysis. As Table 7.5 shows, 91 of our sample were
identified as opioid users. In order to look for any differences between user and
non-user offenders, we looked at these two categories separately. We then
compared their rates of conviction for acquisitive and non-acquisitive offences
between 1970 and 1985. Clearly because of their different ages, convictions
during the 1970s will be based on the older end of the sample. However, as the
age distribution of the two groups is almost identical, there should be no bias.
The results presented in Table 7.5 show that our user-offenders have a quite
different criminal career from non-users, with a dramatic rise in acquisitive
crime convictions during the 1981–5 period. Their non-acquisitive convictions
have risen, but at a much lower rate, especially when compared with the non-
drug-user-offender profile. Our drug-user-offender sample itself divides into
two groups, as Table 7.5 illustrates, in that one third had no criminal record as
juveniles. The emergence of this subgroup of young people is particularly
important. Under normal circumstances, we would not expect a group of
young adults who had passed through the most 'at risk' age period (14–16
years) without coming to official attention for offending, to appear as
recidivists (repeatedly being convicted) in adulthood. Given that they are being
convicted of theft and burglary, and that we know the modal age for the onset

Table 7.5   Mean number of convictions of offenders between 1971 and 1985

	Acquisitive convictions			Non-acquisitive conditions		
	1971–75	1976–80	1981–85	1971–75	1976–80	1981–85
(a) *Offenders known to use opioids against offenders not known to use opioids*						
User-offenders (N = 91)	0.6	1.3	6.0	0.2	1.1	2.1
Non-user-offenders (N = 188)	0.6	1.0	3.4	0.4	1.0	3.1
(b) *User-offenders with no convictions at 16 years against user-offenders with one or more convictions at 16 years*						
User-offenders with record at 16 years (N = 59)	0.9	2.0	6.1	0.3	1.7	2.6
User-offenders with no record at 16 years (N = 32)	0	0.1	5.8	0	0.2	1.2

of heroin use in Wirral is 16–17, it does seem likely that heroin dependency has led this group into regular offending for the first time.

Three groups thus emerge: a non-user-offender 'life of crime' group who have remained criminally active into adulthood; a drug-user-offender group for whom offending pre-dates drug use; and a drug-user group new to offending. All three patterns are in fact atypical in that they mirror neither the relatively crime-free existence of most people nor the temporary 'normal' delinquent career of adolescents formally processed by the police and courts who usually settle down in their late teens. Elsewhere we have plotted these careers based exactly on our data (Parker and Newcombe 1987), but for present purposes it is more useful to consider these career patterns as generalised or archetypical profiles. Figure 7.1 presents four profiles. Profile 1 is our normal delinquent career with settling down occurring in late teens.

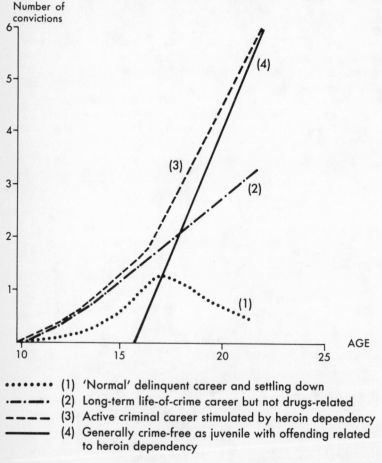

Figure 7.1   Criminal careers and the effect of heroin dependency

Profile 2 is a profile based on our non-user, young adult offender group. This group looks set to mirror the life-of-crime cohort identified in the Home Office (1985) study mentioned earlier. Profile 3 represents a group of young people with criminal convictions as juveniles who may or may not have settled down, but whose heroin dependency has projected them into serious and regular offending and perhaps into a 'life of crime' career of even greater seriousness than the Profile 2 group. Profile 4 is a new-to-crime heroin-dependent group made up of young adults who had been relatively crime-free as juveniles and whose serious and regular offending looks directly related to the onset of heroin use. Their future trajectory seems likely to depend on their drug-taking behaviour although the possibility that they will continue in a criminal mode, even if they give up heroin, obviously remains, given their experiences of imprisonment and the smack subculture.

Users' accounts of financing the heroin habit

We now turn to our second technique for exploring the heroin–crime relationship. Clearly the most likely explanation to have emerged from the last section is that the rise in crime and widespread heroin use are indeed closely related. Even though our user interviews come from a largely independent sample, similar results linking the two phenomena in the same way would be highly persuasive.

Users themselves were in fact unambivalent. A user who is unemployed and needs to 'score' every day has to turn to crime in order to find the money to pay for it, typically, as we pointed out earlier, £20 to £35 per day. Certainly, from the users' point of view, both this fact of life and the chronology involved are quite clear. As Table 7.6 indicates, only 26 per cent reported involvement in crime prior to the onset of heroin use. However, once involved in heroin, as all our sample are or were, the ratios changed dramatically. At the time of interview, 87 per cent admitted to having been directly or indirectly involved in financing their habit illegally and all the sample were in contravention of the Misuse of Drugs Act, which, in the courts' eyes, is a serious offence in itself.

Moreover, even those (13 per cent) who claimed to have refrained, apart from possession offences, from breaking the law, made due acknowledgement

Table 7.6   Self-reportage of offending prior to regular heroin use (per cent)

No criminal activity/convictions	69
Drug offences only	0
Non-drug non-acquisitive only	5
Acquisitive only	7
Drug and acquisitive only	3
Non-drug, non-acquisitive and acquisitive	8
Drug, non-drug, non-acquisitive and acquisitive	3
Not known	5
Total ($N = 61$)	100

to the informal economy associated with occupational 'fiddles' (see also Auld *et al.* 1986) whether they were self-employed or working for a company.

> I used to drive a lorry, y'know, long distances. I was working at that and fiddling me expenses. I mean, everyone fiddled their expenses, but they did it for drink or fun or to pay the mortgage and, instead of me doing it to buy clothes and things for the kids, I was doing it to finance me habit.

As we move across the spectrum, we find (see Table 7.7) a group who were mainly female and relied on the illegal activities of a male partner. We then find a group of user-dealers who financed their habit by supplying heroin to a local network. Significantly, many of these small-time dealers regarded their tactics as less morally reprehensible than stealing or burgling people's houses, not a view shared by the tabloid Press who have labelled 'pushers' as thoroughly evil. As one user put it:

> No, I never stole anything. The thing was, I knew that when people couldn't score, when there were supposed to be a drought on, I could always score. So I could sort of say, if they wanted two grams, I want a quarter for getting it for you. I managed to [support my habit] without burgling and I managed to get quite a lot of gear every day. If I'd had to steal to finance it, I think I'd have just given up.

Moving on to the predominant response, we find that 64 per cent of our sample defined acquisitive crime as their primary source of financing the purchase of heroin, with informants referring to burglary and shoplifting as the main offence categories.

This is unequivocal information and when cross-referenced with our earlier quantitative analysis leaves little room for doubt. The 'extra' crime Wirral has experienced in recent years appears to be closely related to the community's heroin 'epidemic'.

Why should this be the case and why are these findings so conclusive when other researchers have sometimes found a much weaker relationship between the two phenomena (Bennett and Wright 1986a; Hammersley and Morrison 1987)?

Table 7.7 Methods of financing the habit reported by 'known' users* (per cent)

Legal means	13
Dealing	13
Burglary	26
Shoplifting	25
Dealing and burglary	7
Shoplifting and burglary	3
Theft and fraud	3
Illegal activity of others	10
Total (N = 61)	100

*If off heroin at time of interview then last reported method

Criminal and 'smack' subcultures

We have suggested that Wirral's peninsular geography, good public transport system and high-density stable population, coupled with high levels of youth unemployment and social deprivation in its urban townships, provide an ideal backcloth for the rapid spread of heroin use amongst its young. However such conditions are likely to be found in many other urban areas where heroin use has *not* become popular (see Pearson *et al.* 1986). Clearly other ingredients are required. It is perhaps stating the obvious, given what has gone before, to point to the availability of street heroin as the link between the user and crime. What is not so obvious is how, despite draconian measures by the courts and the police, the supply and the price of heroin, although temporarily affected during the 1984–5 police clampdown, have been so stable.

Why have these local heroin supply networks been so resilient? Why have they been, against all the odds, such successful trading mechanisms? The answer is to be found in the cultural history and socio-economic make-up of the region's unskilled working-class community. This community has throughout the century stood at the interface between the 'straight' and alternative economies, relying more on the one in times of prosperity and well-paid jobs, and the other in times of hardship and job scarcity (see also Box 1987). The massive unemployment in the region during the 1980s has seen an increasing reliance amongst Wirral's largely unemployed townships upon the alternative economy. The presence of large numbers of people daily rummaging through the borough's rubbish disposal tips and the growth of pawnbrokers and second-hand shops in downtown areas bear witness to this. This informal economy also crosses over legal boundaries to encompass those who will accept stolen goods and condone the local criminal subculture. These traditional subcultural agreements which link 'respectable' and criminal lifestyles flourish in Wirral's urban townships and municipal estates. Indeed without them many poor families would not be able to cope.

However, a hidden cost of these traditional arrangements, for the neighbourhoods and communities which maintain them, is that they have facilitated the local heroin trade. They have, unintentionally in the main, provided the bulk of users with a means of converting crime into cash. Furthermore, this cash is then exchanged upwards into the hands of the often non-drug-using heroin dealer and from there into the national distribution system which is part of the international heroin economy.

Once again the evidence for this conclusion comes from a mixture of our two methodological approaches. Our investigation of criminal records and known drug users allowed us to look at the areas of residence of our 300 sample offenders. Given that they were selected for a wide range of offending categories we can assume they are representative of Wirral's offender population. In Chapter 2 we identified the area of residence by township of up to 1,600 drug users. We undertook the same exercise for our sample of 300, distributing them across Wirral's 48 townships. The proportions of these offenders in each township population are significantly positively correlated with the proportions of problem drug users in each township ($r = 0.6$,

$p<0.001$). It appears that, in the main, opioid users and young offenders live in the same residential areas. These results are consistent with findings in the United States and Sweden, where it is increasingly the case that drug users and criminals come from the same areas (Fry 1985).

Although it is important to demonstrate that our new heroin users and regular property offenders live side by side, the most persuasive evidence that illicit heroin supplies have been sustained by utilising traditional subcultural arrangements comes from our ethnographic work.

The link between 'straight' ordinary people and local heroin dealers will obviously vary through time and location. The dynamics of the heroin trade are clearly enormously complex (see Whittaker 1986; and Johnson et al. 1985) and we can only offer a crude outline here of what has been occurring in this particular community. Clearly this local picture needs linking into the, as yet missing, analysis of the national distribution system and the formal economy.

The presence of the 'straights', the coping poor of a region, particularly in recession and decline, is a prerequisite. The trading system or chain needs customers who will strike a bargain on the doorstep or in the local pub for something they want or need, be it a video recorder or a frozen chicken, a leather jacket or a radio cassette player. For the majority of these customers receiving stolen goods, this is their only transaction in the distribution system and they have no contact with heroin whatsoever. For them, taking the opportunity to supplement their often low standard of living seems common sense not crime. They would not recognise their activities as doing any harm or being criminal and their transactions are comparable with 'fiddles' which take place at all levels of society (see Ditton 1977; Box 1987).

It is with this large potential market that the majority of our new heroin users, the 'smackheads', do their business and again there is no need for heroin to be alluded to. Most often our small-time user is merely trying to sell something he's stolen from a shop or house. He will be confident, because of these arrangements in his community, that his sales techniques will neither cause offence nor put him at risk of being 'blown up' and consequently arrested.

> I sell things to people, like. Y'know, you can sell anything around here. If it's a bargain, or something for the house, women'll buy it. I've sold videos, boxes of toilet rolls. Anything.

Alternatively our small-time user might approach a local fence or receiver who also has nothing to do with drugs. Again neither side is likely to taboo this transaction. Having moved his stolen property, cash in hand, our user will contact one of a number of local user-dealers or 'bag men'. The bag man is probably at the limit between acceptable and unacceptable behaviour in his own community, in that his connection with heroin will damn him in some people's eyes. However, because he lives locally and his activities are largely with other known individuals, the community will also turn a blind eye to this transaction and only its being detected independently by the police will stop it. The bag man is likely to have his own heroin habit which he finances by small-time dealing. He buys a gram at £60 and sells wraps or bags at £5. He might cut 25 bags from a gram, which gives him a profit of about £65, enough to finance his own and/or a partner's habit.

Obviously the bag man might 'move up' a rung or two and deal for profit, but most do not. Instead they 'service' a very local network of users who know each other and indeed who are part of the local scene. This 'natural' network, submerged into everyday community life, offers considerable camouflage for these transactions.

Beyond the bag men are the 'breadheads'. They are unlikely to be accepted by elders and parents in neighbourhoods with heroin 'problems' (Dorn *et al.* 1987). Instead they will seek 'safe houses' in 'quiet' places or in the high-rise blocks where anonymity is almost guaranteed. The breadhead is more concerned with money than heroin. He is the classic example of the user or non-user criminal on the make. He may 'lay on', that is, give, heroin on credit to bag men. This process links the lower level user-dealer firmly into the heroin-crime cycle since any 'weakness' on his part, whereby he uses more smack than this 'business' will allow, brings him into debt with the breadhead. To avoid the possibility of hassle or violent retribution the bag man must turn to crime.

> There were also some people that were selling gear that weren't smackheads and they'd do you a lay-on without any rings or surety or nothing and you'd say, 'Well, lay us on half a gram and I'll sell it', and they'd say, 'Alright'. And then you'd go back a couple of days later and say: 'Look, I haven't got the money. Lay me on another half a gram.' In the end, you'd owe them a couple of grams and you'd have to go shoplifting in Chester or somewhere because you couldn't go down town in case they were there.

The breadhead who services the bag men is potentially into quite big business. The following informant, for instance, dealt in ounces on a daily basis.

> I was getting smack for, like, £900 [an ounce]. A lot of people were paying £1,300 for theirs, like, but I was regular and getting it for £900. I was selling it in grams, £60 a gram. I was doing grams to people and they were doing it out in [£5] bags. I'd keep a certain person, like, seven grams and he'd come and get a gram and, when he came back with the bread, I'd do him another one. He'd only get 12 bags from a gram, 'cos he'd smoke the rest. If you did the whole gram out in bags, you'd do 25 to 30 bags.

This local level of the heroin distribution network has not been a new and sinister creation set up from outside but an adaptation of long-established trading mechanisms which were already central to the irregular economy. Many of our new heroin users were integrated into this system long before their heroin habit determined their lifestyle, as their criminal records show. Nevertheless, it is the need to finance their habit which has triggered an economic boom and accelerated trading in this area. Although activity has expanded at all levels it is at the base of the 'system' that we find the most new activity and effort. It is with the 'straights', the smackheads and the bag men that the local business cycle has boomed. Whilst not all users are busy people and whilst many sometime busy users will burn out or have periods of lethargy, we should be clear that 'taking care of business' produces a lifestyle of considerable energy and imagination.

Doing the business

Although officially unemployed, whether prior to or because of heroin use, the user is in fact very busy. 'Doing the business' becomes his new occupation and indeed preoccupation. A circular structure increasingly determines his or her every day. There is no inevitable starting point but the process, once in motion, feeds upon itself. The user wants to 'score', at best to get high, and at worst because he's 'strung out', but most likely because he's trying to avoid 'turkey'. But to 'score' you need money, to get money you must commit crime.

> I'd wake up in the morning pretty early, about 8 o'clock, feeling pretty rough. No matter how much smack I'd had the day before, I'd always wake up feeling pretty rough, just get dressed, whizz out, head for the nearest shopping area and sort of try and make as much money as I could. Y'know, sort of get as much gear from the shops as I could. Then sell it, go and score, smoke what I'd scored and go shoplifting again.

Obviously, in reality, the drugs career of a single user or a user couple living together produces a rich variety of strategies for coping with 'the cycle'. New contingencies can intervene, such as a court hearing, a period in custody, a local heroin drought or an unexpected windfall. Overall, however, this user's day can be seen as the predominant timetable and approach: the thread which runs through the majority of user histories. This dangerous lifestyle appears similar to that described by Preble and Casey (1969) as 'taking care of business' and by Hanson et al. (1985) in their study of inner-city heroin users in the United States. As yet the comparable urban English user life cycle seems less violent and less subcultural than that in the United States. However, as the trend of official responses seems remarkably similar there are grounds for believing that further transformations are likely.

A crime control disaster

We must now turn to the implications, for Wirral, of the wheeling and dealing around heroin, discussed in the last section. If we make the conservative estimate that about 3,000 users are looking for £20 worth of heroin a day, we are describing a local heroin market worth about £22 million a year. Obviously by no means all of this is financed through acquisitive crime: we have pointed to legitimate employment and the user-dealer solution as other important avenues. Nevertheless, the increase in acquisitive crime documented earlier is a by-product of extensive heroin use and is a measure of the price the community at large has had to pay.

The most potent example of this concerns the dramatic increase in domestic burglaries, whereby some 11,000 households in the Borough of Wirral are broken into each year. Many victims are from the well-heeled suburbs but as many again are from the deprived townships where most users reside and where fuel slot meters and cash rather than credit cards still prevail. However, no matter what the social class of the victim, the emotional cost to the individual can be enormous,[3] and the damage to community solidarity invidious.

As we noted in Chapter 1, the initial 'common-sense' response to the heroin 'epidemic' and accompanying quasi-moral panic was to apply the tactic of heavy policing and punitive sentencing. This approach fitted both the dominant politics of law and order propagated by central government and the mood of the local Establishment. Consequently between 1984 and 1986 the police and courts were extremely vigilant and highly active in dealing with those committing either drugs offences or offences related to financing dependency. The borough was the subject of an unprecedented 'clampdown' when the drugs squad, alongside especially deployed police officers, carried out a major exercise in arresting drug users and user-dealers. An exceptional number of raids were carried out on suspects' homes within the area. Moreover, local magistrates courts have, throughout the period, taken quite draconian measures in locking up, or committing to Crown Court, several hundred people found guilty of committing drugs-related crimes. Indeed, far from being a plea of mitigation, the discovery of a heroin habit has been the trigger which has led so many user-offenders into custody, both during remand and after sentence. Wise users now deliberately attempt to hide their drug use from local officials, believing that the police, probation officers and court officials cannot be trusted with such information.

This clampdown, whilst not a response to a social construction which falsified the size of the 'problem' (see Cohen 1973), was always going to produce unintended consequences, because it misconstrued both the nature of the 'problem' and the impact of punitive policing. First, even leaving aside widespread drug use in prison, locking up drug user-offenders has a low success rate in the production of either law-abiding citizens or drug-free individuals. Second, the impact of the police clampdown, without infinite resources, could only be ephemeral. Thus whilst the police campaign undoubtedly produced a localised heroin 'drought' during 1985, as well as taking a large number of small-time user-dealers and a few big fish out of circulation for some time, the price of street heroin has not increased and its availability remains good for the user who knows where to look. What occurred in the first instance was a displacement of supply sites whereby, although some Wirral users may have turned to treatment or even moved away, the majority went outside the borough to score. Since towns and neighbourhoods throughout the whole region were the locations of heroin outbreaks, Wirral users were able to do their business elsewhere, particularly in Liverpool. Moreover, given finite police resources and changing priorities, new trading sites sprung up and unrecognised outlets continued undisturbed.

These ever-fluid local supply networks come and go. Not surprisingly, therefore, during 1987, with the heat off them, Wirral's own networks were in the process of recovering and reopening, and in some cases offering new drugs. Interestingly, though, many Wirral users continued and preferred to score away from their home base, having developed a customer loyalty to regular 'business' arrangements elsewhere.

The iron-fist approach to heroin networks might well 'work' at the very beginning of a micro-epidemic when small numbers and users new to the drug are involved. The whole 'contagious' network can be broken down and users treated rapidly (Hughes 1977). However it is not usually possible to identify outbreaks at this stage (Dorn et al. 1987). More typically, as has been the case in Wirral, micro-outbreaks spread into a full-scale 'epidemic', by means of the activities of new users and before official responses could be activated. The heavy law-and-order response composed by central government and operated in classic style in Wirral came some three years into the 'epidemic'. It seems that, on balance, the approach, as well as being enormously costly in terms of police, court, probation and prison budgets, has been largely ineffective. It has not closed down the heroin distribution networks nor reduced crime. What it has done is criminalise and imprison a large population of, predominantly young men and women and, by the police's own admission (Merseyside Police 1986), driven the whole drugs scene underground. The amplification process described by Young (1974) and others had been classically reconstructed and the failure of the approach matches international experience (Palombi 1984).

There are, then, no clear winners except perhaps for the new drugs service — professionals, like ourselves, whose work is in demand. Basically Wirral remains strongly victimised in relation to crime and the presence of an increasingly subcultural heroin world. Users have themselves been criminalised and their families have had to try and cope with seeing their sons and daughters get ever deeper into the penal system. Many heroin families are in grief. Yet neither side of the equation has been helped by the official law-and-order response.

This is not to suggest that we have the solution to this scenario. We do not. The situation looks increasingly endemic rather than epidemic, structural rather than superficial. In particular, we should not ignore the attractions of the deviant lifestyles in which users have become immersed. Being a 'smackhead' has potential attractions for all youth but particularly for the unemployed surplus youth to be found in Wirral's recession-hit urban areas. For them the commitment to conventional lifestyle is strained or made tenuous by their lowly socio-economic position and the fact that coping strategies of an illegal nature are, as we have described already, condoned in their neighbourhood, particularly in the absence of legal ones. That these illegal pathways have both presented heroin as attractive and sustained reasonable supplies of acceptable quality adds to the *possibility* that regular use will occur. The motivation to begin usage is obviously still required and, as we have noted in earlier chapters, is usually of a very 'ordinary' nature, being based on curiosity or an extension of a repertoire of drug use, usually with the encouragement of a friend or partner.

Once into the role of regular user and with the initial legal options running out, the heroin–crime lifestyle emerges for the majority. It is a complex mixture of choice and constraint, good times and bad. Its attractions are those of the subculture: structures which 'arise as attempts to resolve collectively experienced problems arising from contradictions in the social structure' (Brake 1980). The nature of these contradictions for the new heroin users wil obviously depend on how they perceive the social processes we have documented — their lack of educational qualifications and employment opportunities which can provide the legal purchase of the good times. However, in general, once 'into' being a regular user, choice becomes more constrained. Users may be rejected by parents, and imprisoned with little warning, so that they become 'unemployable' as well as unemployed. The exits on the roundabout are closed off and the pace quickens so that, whilst becoming a 'smackhead' was easy, giving up the status or role is not. Add to this users' physical and psychological dependence upon the drug and it is not hard to see why the heroin–crime relationship is becoming a structural feature in this community. Because of this we cannot have a neat ending. The career patterns of the new heroin users are still unfolding but, in the context of high unemployment, recession and an ever-increasing reliance on imprisonment as part of a failing law-and-order strategy (Box 1987), we should not expect much change in the immediate future. For this community, talk of solutions and 'stamping out the problem' through forthright policing is increasingly muted. It is now more a question of learning to live with and minimise the costs of the heroin-crime spiral.

In Chapter 8 we focus on adolescents and survey the present and next generation of young people, who are apparently most at risk of swelling the ranks of the new drug users. We return to our attempts to forecast which sections of Wirral's 'ordinary' young people, be they at school, at college or on work experience schemes, are most likely to use drugs.

Notes

1 Only 50 of the 300 people in the sample had one or more Misuse of Drugs Act convictions, compared to 273 with one or more convictions for acquisitive offences, and 214 with one or more convictions for non-acquisitive offences. These 50 people had been convicted of a total of 95 Misuse of Drugs Act offences — about half had only one such conviction and about a quarter had two such convictions. The vast majority (77) of the 95 Misuse of Drugs Act offences committed were possession offences, nine were supply offences, and nine were other Misuse of Drugs Act offences (e.g. cultivation). Only nine of the 95 Misuse of Drugs Act offences were identified as involving opioids, most of the other cases being non specific as to type of drug. As might be expected, the proportion of 'known' drug user offenders with one or more Misuse of Drugs Act convictions was far higher than the corresponding proportion for offenders not on the register of known drug users (33 per cent against 8 per cent). Finally, a far higher proportion of the burglary group (27 per cent) and

the theft group (15 per cent) had one or more Misuse of Drugs Act convictions, compared to the UTMV or car-taking group (10 per cent) and the criminal damage group (6 per cent).

2 Chi-squared tests reveal significantly different frequencies of known drug users among the four groups of offenders (χ^2 = 21.4, df = 3, $p<0.001$), and of known opioid users among the four groups of offenders (χ^2 = 25.5, df = 3, $p<0.001$). Examination of the components of the χ^2 statistic reveals that this effect is largely accounted for by the burglary offenders and the criminal damage offenders:

	Known drug users	Known opioid users
Theft	0.15	0.02
Burglary	10.95	12.19
UTMV	1.23	1.86
Criminal damage	9.08	11.59

3 One of our key recommendations to Wirral Council, in a report on the heroin–crime relationship, was that they set up a victim support scheme.

8

Heroin in perspective: drug use among young people in Wirral

In the previous four chapters, we have examined the very considerable social costs of heroin for users, their families, and the wider community. We have tried to show how these costs derive mainly from the illegality of heroin and the lack of purchasing power of the new users. Thus, society's repressive policies towards heroin play a major role in the production of such problems as the use of contaminated drugs, stealing from relatives, being thrown out of home, burgling, shoplifting, drug dealing, spread of disease, being convicted and imprisoned, losing 'straight' friends, avoiding contact with official agencies, the formation of 'smackhead' subcultures — in short, the marginalisation of users.

However, it is not meant to imply that heroin, even heroin which is not heavily 'cut' with adulterants, is harmless. All drugs are potentially dangerous, depending on how society controls them and how the individual uses them. No doubt if heroin were made legal and freely available, with no changes in care, treatment or education policies, there would be a very considerable casualty rate (overdoses, accidents, spread of infection, and so on). Individuals, because of their different social and psychological characteristics, will experience and react to different drugs, be they alcohol, heroin, cannabis, or even caffeine, in an enormous variety of ways. Heroin, perhaps more than any other illegal drug, has not been fairly appraised in relation to its effects on the individual and society. It has instead become a potent symbol of the danger and disorder which contemporary British society faces. We will see in Chapter 9 how this powerful mythology which surrounds heroin has handicapped the guardians of Wirral's official responses. Wirral's reaction is a microcosm of our society's pervasive 'war against drugs' mentality, a confused and hypocritical response epitomised by the government's 'Heroin Screws You Up' campaign, and by other educational interventions aimed at 'stamping out' illicit drug use.

Education about drugs: truth or propaganda?

One major 'battleground' in the 'war against drugs' has been the educational arena. This has involved attempts to reduce youthful experimentation with drugs by deploying four general types of campaign or educational programme (see Swadi and Zeitlin 1987, for a recent assessment): fear-arousal or 'shock-horror' approaches, which aim to scare people into not taking drugs; informational or factual approaches, which assume that selected facts will be enough to put people off the idea of taking drugs; person-orientated approaches, which aim to strengthen the personal dispositions and attitudes associated with abstinence from drugs, such as self-esteem and conformity; and situation-orientated approaches, which aim to train people in the rational decision-making skills necessary to resist offers of drugs in the situations in which they are commonly encountered (such as parties).

However, it might be expected that these approaches could, at best, only have limited success, if we acknowledge a number of social-psychological facts: young people often like taking risks; information which is not relevant to people's desires and plans will usually be ignored; personality traits are difficult to modify even with intensive therapy, and the relationship between attitudes and behaviour is complex and unpredictable; and rational consideration of choices may lead to the decision to try a drug rather than 'just say no', and, in any case, affective (emotional) states often determine behaviour — that is, people frequently behave irrationally. Other important factors which determine the effectiveness of drug education, but which have often been neglected, include how the 'message' is presented, who presents it, and the age group at which it is targeted.

Indeed, it is now widely acknowledged that school-based education programmes which have tried to deter young people from taking illegal drugs have generally been ineffective, and sometimes counterproductive (for references to several major reviews of evaluation studies, see Dorn 1981; Home Office, 1984; *British Medical Journal* 1985; Newcombe 1987a). It appears that 'primary prevention' programmes are irrelevant to the majority of young people who are not likely to take illegal drugs, and are ineffective in the case of the minority who are potential users of illegal drugs.

These conclusions are mirrored by the findings of research into the government's high-profile anti-heroin advertisements in the mass media during 1985, the main target of which were 'young people who have not tried heroin but who are potentially at risk' (RBL 1986). The 'Heroin Screws You Up' campaign had all the basic ingredients of the heavily discredited 'shock-horror' approach, with posters and television adverts depicting the misery of zombie-like youths with acne and greasy hair. Strangely, it was undertaken against the advice of the government's own experts, the Advisory Council on the Misuse of Drugs, and it has been described by many seasoned researchers and practitioners in the field as being more like propaganda than education (see, for example, Plant 1986).

The research commissioned by the government to evaluate the campaign found no difference between the proportions of 13–20-year-olds using heroin or intending to use heroin before and after the initiation of the campaign (about 1 per cent). However, the research findings showed that, while attitudes to heroin had become more negative among young people who were unlikely to have or want access to it, attitudes among those most likely to have to choose became more pro-heroin. For instance, among young people who knew heroin users — that is, the main target group of the campaign — 52 per cent believed that heroin was more dangerous than cannabis before the campaign, but only 42 per cent believed this after the campaign (RBL 1986, p. 38). Although the relationship between attitudes and behaviour is far from simple, the significance of these findings is reflected in a *British Medical Journal* editorial (1985, p. 416) at the time of the campaign:

> What ministers in London and Edinburgh should realise (and they have been told) is that unemployed youngsters on Merseyside do no react in the same way to exaggerated drug campaigns in the media as do their middle-aged constituents in Rushcliffe and Argyle and Bute.

Furthermore, the campaign was mounted with insufficient forethought as to whether other forms of drug use were more prevalent and therefore more deserving of attention than heroin, and to whether heroin was more or less harmful than the other drugs — legal or illegal — to which young people may have access. Indeed, the 'war against heroin' mentality of the government campaign, and of the mass media in general, could well have misled some young people not only into believing that heroin use was a widespread illicit activity among their peers (thus giving it all the attractions of 'forbidden fruit'), but, more seriously, could have deflected attention from the fact that other drugs can be equally or more harmful.

Interestingly, at the same time as the campaign, many professionals who worked closely with heroin users and other drug takers were beginning to express discontent about the myths perpetuated by the mass media and official campaigns concerning drugs (see, for example, Kay 1986). There was an increasing feeling that the time had come for an end to the hypocrisy of a society which allows alcohol and tobacco advertisements alongside 'Heroin Screws You Up' posters, and which often implies that illegal drug use typically leads to death (when it in fact kills 200–300 people a year) while vigorously promoting tobacco (which kills about 100,000 a year). Such reform would require a sweeping away of the mythology which obscures our understanding of the causes and effects of psychoactive drug use, and a more accurate appraisal of heroin, putting it on an equal evaluative footing with alcohol, tobacco, tranquillisers, cannabis and all of society's 'drugs of solace' (Cameron and Jones 1985). As Malyon (1986, p. 9) puts it, 'the key to any fresh approach towards drug use and abuse is acceptance of the fact that humankind has been using a bewildering array of mind-bending substances since the dawn of civilisation and is unlikely to change its ways'.

With these considerations in mind, we decided to evaluate heroin within the broader context of general drug-taking in Wirral, that is, as just one of the available products in the contemporary 'drugs supermarket'. A survey of the use of legal and illegal drugs in Wirral's general youth population enabled us to compare the prevalence of heroin use with the prevalence of other forms of drug-taking, and also to establish what characteristics are associated with various forms of drug use, including regular use of illegal drugs. The findings of this survey, reported in the next section, suggest that national and local drug education programmes have been less than effective in discouraging drug-taking among Wirral youth. However, it should be noted that, although these surveys were conducted following the initial phase of the government's anti-heroin campaign, they cannot be used to evaluate the campaign's effects in Wirral, because there is no accurate information about levels of heroin use and other drug-taking *before* the campaign.

A survey of drug use among young people in Wirral

It is now well documented that people usually first become interested in mind-altering substances during their teenage years. In order to gauge the extent and nature of teenage drug involvement in Wirral, taking into account that constraints on time and resources precluded the possibility of investigating even a 5 per cent random sample of Wirral's 30,000 15–20-year-olds, we decided to conduct separate surveys of young people in three different occupational groups: senior secondary schoolchildren, college students, and a group of young people on a Youth Training Scheme (a one-year occupational programme for unemployed teenagers). The information was collected by self-report questionnaires, which consisted mainly of multiple-choice answers. Although there were a number of specific variations in questions between the three questionnaires, which arose from the need to tailor each questionnaire to the three different groups of young people surveyed, the questionnaires shared a common three-section format. The first section contained general questions about respondents' social characteristics. The second section contained questions about their experiences of 'licit drugs', that is, drugs which are legally available and whose use is socially sanctioned (namely, alcohol and tobacco). The final section contained questions about respondents' experiences of illicit drugs, that is, drugs which it is illegal to possess or supply, or drugs which it is generally legal to possess or supply but which receive society's disapproval (such as solvents and magic mushrooms).

The questionnaires were completed by groups of young people in teaching rooms, usually (but not always) with the tutor having left the room. Although efforts were made to dissuade respondents from conferring, preventing communication in some of the groups was not possible without risking a loss of goodwill and co-operation. Consequently, it was possible that some of the respondents may have falsely admitted to taking drugs because their friends had done so or because they thought it was in some way desirable. However, this bias was likely to be outweighed, or at least offset, by respondents' failure to disclose drug use due to fear of identification and punishment. In order to minimise such false denials, we adopted a number of procedures to assure respondents of total confidentiality: no name, address or other identifying information was required; respondents were told that they did not have to answer any questions that they did not want to answer; they were promised that no information about individual responses would be given to teachers or employers; and all respondents were given an envelope in which to seal up their completed questionnaires before handing them back to the researcher.

The first survey involved 268 people age 16–20 years who were employed by a large company in Birkenhead as trainees on a Youth Training Scheme (YTS) programme (or as apprentices in 49 cases). Questionnaires were completed by small groups in 13 weekly sessions between November 1985 and February 1986. The second survey, of 198 young people aged 15–16 years, was conducted during one week in March 1986 in six of Wirral's 26 state secondary schools. Permission was gained from the Education Department to survey one fifth-year class of average educational ability in two schools in an area of high social deprivation, two in an area of low social deprivation, and two in an area of medium social deprivation. The schools in the areas of high and medium social deprivation were comprehensives, with the 'low' area being represented by a grammar school and a secondary modern school. Three of the schools were co-educational, and three were single-sex schools (two boys' schools and one girls' school). It was intended to survey about 30 pupils at each school, although only 18 were surveyed in one of the schools in an area of high social deprivation (because of truancy), and 60 were surveyed in the secondary modern school at the request of the headmaster.

The third survey of 225 people, of whom 86 per cent were aged 16–19 years, was conducted over two days in November 1986 at each of the three sites of Wirral Metropolitan College. A representative 10 per cent sample of the full-time student population was approximated by surveying classes of second-year students from 13 major courses, one or two from each of the college's nine departments (depending on their size). The size of the classes surveyed varied between ten and 35 students.

In sum, we surveyed a total of 691 young people in three occupational groups, the vast majority of whom were between 15 and 20 years of age.

Main findings

Characteristics of the sample
Almost all the YTS trainees were male, compared with 61 per cent of the schoolchildren and 51 per cent of the college students. All of the

schoolchildren were resident in Wirral, compared with 93 per cent of the students and 82 per cent of the trainees (most of the non-Wirral respondents were living in Liverpool). All but one of the schoolchildren and over 90 per cent of the students were single, childless and living with their parent(s).

Pupils and students were also asked about their parents' occupational status. Unemployment among men in Wirral stood at 24 per cent in 1985, which is similar to the unemployment rate among the fathers of the schoolchildren (20 per cent), but over twice as high as the unemployment rate among students' fathers (10 per cent). This suggests that the college students are more likely to come from families in the higher socio-economic groups. In the sample of schoolchildren, the highest rates of unemployment were found among fathers of pupils attending the two schools in areas of high social deprivation (39 per cent and 33 per cent) in comparison with the fathers of pupils attending the two schools in areas of low social deprivation (3 per cent and 15 per cent). This confirms the validity of the selection of these schools as representative of areas of high, medium and low social deprivation.

Use of alcohol

The vast majority of the young people surveyed drank alcohol on a regular or occasional basis: 92 per cent of the schoolchildren, 92 per cent of the YTS trainees, and 96 per cent of the college students. Regular drinking (once a week or more) was reported by 47 per cent of the schoolchildren, 72 per cent of the trainees, and 74 per cent of the students. Daily drinking was reported by less than 2 per cent of the respondents (and by no schoolchildren). Overall, the typical drinking frequency was between one and four times a month for the schoolchildren, and one to three times a week for YTS trainees and students.

The majority of respondents expressed a preference for beer (including lager or cider), although there were clear sex differences. About nine in ten males preferred beer to other alcoholic beverages, whereas female preferences were more evenly divided between beer and liqueurs/aperitifs, and also spirits in the case of female students (sex differences are more fully discussed later in this chapter). Respondents were also asked to state how much of their preferred beverage they drank in a typical drinking session, and about four-fifths gave a figure; these were coded according to standard units of alcohol (half a pint of beer, one measure of spirits, or one glass of wine or liqueur being each equivalent to one unit). The typical quantity of alcohol consumed per drinking occasion was about three to six units by schoolchildren, eight to 12 units by YTS trainees, and three to six units by college students. The YTS trainees were clearly the heaviest drinkers, with 27 per cent stating that they drank between 13 and 20 units of alcohol per session, compared with 7 per cent of the schoolchildren and 6 per cent of the students. This difference could be due to the fact that the YTS sample is comprised almost entirely of males (who showed a tendency to drink more per session than females in the other groups), or to the fact that the YTS survey was conducted during the Christmas holiday period. Nevertheless, heavy drinking is a widely recognised characteristic of young males in manual employment (see Plant et al. 1985). Another measure of excessive drinking was overdosing: 57 per cent of the schoolchildren and 69 per cent of the students stated that they had experienced a hangover.

The average age at which respondents first tried alcohol was reported as 11 years by schoolchildren, 14 years by YTS trainees, and 13 years by students. Since the schoolchildren are the youngest group, this may reflect an age-based reporting effect rather than a tendency towards earlier drinking, although the latter possibility is consistent with the impressions of teachers in the schools surveyed.

The main reasons for drinking alcohol given by all three groups of young people were pleasure (including enjoyment, relaxation, fun and getting drunk) and being sociable (including 'mixing' in pubs and clubs, being with/like friends). About 4 per cent of the respondents stated that they wanted to give up drinking alcohol, usually for financial reasons.

Use of tobacco
Up to four in ten of the 691 young people surveyed smoked cigarettes (or cigars or pipes in a few cases) on a regular or occasional basis: 40 per cent of the schoolchildren, 38 per cent of the YTS trainees, and 36 per cent of the college students. About half of the non-smoking pupils and students were former smokers, as were about a third of the non-smoking trainees.

Not all smokers were daily users: about a third of the school smokers used on an occasional (non-daily) basis, compared with a sixth of the smoking students and about 5 per cent of the smoking trainees. It seems likely that more of the school smokers had just begun to smoke and had not yet escalated to a daily habit. The average number of cigarettes smoked by daily smokers was about six to ten per day, although the YTS trainees displayed a tendency towards heavier smoking.

The average age at which the young people first tried cigarettes was 13 years in the case of the YTS trainees, and 11 years in the case of schoolchildren. As in the case of alcohol, further investigation would be needed to establish whether this difference accurately reflects an earlier onset of smoking among Wirral's young people or whether it is the result of an age-based reporting effect. The main reason given for smoking was pleasure (enjoyment, relaxation), followed by dependence. In sharp contrast to the small proportion of drinkers wanting to give up alcohol, about six in ten of the smokers wanted to give up smoking (61 per cent of pupils and 62 per cent of students), primarily for health reasons, followed by financial reasons.

Past use of illicit drugs
Schoolchildren and students were asked whether they had been offered or had ever tried each of seven types of illicit drug — cannabis, magic mushrooms, solvents, LSD, amphetamines, heroin and cocaine — and to list any other drugs they had tried. However, YTS trainees were asked the multiple-choice question only for cannabis and heroin, although they were also asked to list any other drugs they had tried. Overall, 40 per cent of the schoolchildren, 43 per cent of the college students, and 37 per cent of the YTS trainees had tried one or more illicit drugs.

The most popular illicit drug was clearly cannabis, which had been tried by three or four out of every ten of the young people surveyed (Table 8.1). The next most frequently used illicit drugs overall are magic mushrooms, tried by one in every six or seven of the respondents. However, amphetamines were more popular among the students (tried by about one in six), and was also the third most frequently used drug by YTS trainees. By contrast, solvents were used by a far higher proportion of schoolchildren compared with the other groups. Only 2.5 per cent of the respondents reported having tried heroin (17 out of 691), and less than 1 per cent had tried other drugs. However, failure to disclose drug use may have been higher in the case of heroin and cocaine, since these items consistently received a higher non-response rate than other drug items (up to 30 per cent in the survey of schoolchildren).

Table 8.1   Illicit drug offers and use among three groups of young people (per cent)

| | Schoolchildren | | | YTS trainees | | | College students | | |
	Nev	Ref	Try	Nev	Ref	Try	Nev	Ref	Try
Cannabis	48	16	36	35	33	32	32	30	39
Mushrooms	64	19	17	*	*	14	59	27	14
Solvents	70	13	17	*	*	3	77	13	10
Amphetamines	82	10	8	*	*	11	65	18	17
LSD	80	12	9	*	*	*	70	19	11
Cocaine	93	4	3	*	*	*	82	15	4
Heroin	89	8	3	75	22	3	84	14	2
Others	96	2	2	*	*	1	99	1	0

*No data available
Key: Nev = never offered/not stated   Ref = offered but refused
       Try = have tried the drug

Of those respondents offered each drug, the highest numbers of acceptors were found in the case of cannabis: 69 per cent of schoolchildren, 48 per cent of YTS trainees, and 56 per cent of students offered cannabis had tried it. By contrast, the lowest numbers of acceptors were found in the case of heroin: 25 per cent of schoolchildren, 11 per cent of YTS trainees and 14 per cent of students offered heroin had tried it. Between a third and a half of the young people offered other drugs had tried them.

Finally, students and YTS trainees were also asked which drugs they had used in the month up to the survey. Nine per cent of the YTS trainees and 12 per cent of the students had used cannabis, and 4 per cent of students had used amphetamines in the previous month, but only 1 or 2 per cent in each group had used any other drugs during the same period.

The validity of responses to drug-use questions was investigated only in the case of college students, by employing the 'honesty question' suggested in the World Health Organisation's 'Methodology for Student Drug-Use Surveys' (Smart et al. 1980). That is, students who indicated that they had never tried any illegal drugs were asked: 'If you had tried any illegal drugs, do you think that you would have admitted it in this questionnaire?'. Of the 127 students who indicated that they had never tried any illegal drug, only nine (7 per cent) stated that they would not have admitted it if they had, although a further 19 (15 per cent) indicated that they were 'not sure', and seven (6 per cent) did not answer the question. Thus, if we assume that all 35 of these students had tried illegal drugs but were not willing to admit it, we can calculate that the proportion of college students who had tried illegal drugs may have been underestimated by up to 16 per cent, giving a maximum try-rate among students of 59 per cent. It should also be noted that truancy in some schools, especially those in areas of high social deprivation, may have produced an underestimate of drug-trying among the schoolchildren.

Regular drug use
Regular illicit drug use (typically once a month or more) stood at 10 per cent among the schoolchildren, 20 per cent among the YTS trainees, and 11 per cent among the college students (14 per cent of the overall sample). Although there were minor differences between definitions of regular use in the three surveys, two general types of regular use were discernible: cannabis only, or cannabis and a secondary drug. The vast majority of regular users among trainees and students were using cannabis only, whereas almost half of the regular users still at school (nine respondents) were also using another drug, typically amphetamines. Only six respondents (four trainees, one student, and one pupil) reported being regular users of heroin, although just two used it more than once a week (both YTS trainees).

About two-thirds of the regular cannabis users smoked it less than once a week, and approximately a quarter used cannabis on a weekly basis. Daily use was reported by one in seven of the cannabis users in the YTS group, and by one in six of the school-age users, but by no students.

Over half of the regular drug users in each of the three samples stated that their main reason for taking drugs was pleasure (including fun, relaxation, and intoxication). The other common reasons given were preferring the drug (typically cannabis) to other drugs such as alcohol, curiosity, boredom, changing awareness, and coping with anxiety or depression. No regular drug users mentioned dependence as a reason for using drugs, which contrasts sharply with the many cigarette smokers who stated that they smoked from habit. Futhermore, only one user among the 24 regular drug users in the college sample stated that he wanted to give up (amphetamines, for health reasons), compared with six in ten of the smokers. However, these differences may have arisen because these young people had usually been smoking cigarettes for a much longer period than they had been using illicit drugs.

Intended drug use
Young people in the school and college samples were also asked about their intentions to use illicit drugs in the future. More specifically, they were asked to indicate, for each of the seven drugs, one of four intentions: I will never take it, I have not yet decided, I might take it, and I will take it. Table 8.2 shows the proportions of respondents indicating each intention, excluding non-respondents (see Parker *et al.* 1986c, for details). As in the cases of past drug

use and regular drug use, the illicit drug most likely to be used in the future was
cannabis: 24 per cent of schoolchildren and 30 per cent of college students
stated that they might or will use cannabis. The drugs next most likely to be
used by these young people in the future were magic mushrooms in the case of
schoolchildren (16 per cent) and amphetamines in the case of college students
(13 per cent). In addition, about one in ten of the schoolchildren said they
might or would use amphetamines and LSD, and about one in twelve of the
college students might or would use magic mushrooms. The two drugs least
likely to be used were heroin and cocaine in the case of schoolchildren, and
heroin and solvents in the case of college students.

Table 8.2   Intended drug use among two groups of young people (per cent)

	Fifth-year schoolchildren				College students			
	Never	Undec.	Might	Will	Never	Undec.	Might	Will
Cannabis	69	6	16	8	63	7	16	14
Mushrooms	80	4	9	7	86	6	7	1
Amphetamines	87	3	5	4	83	4	9	4
LSD	87	3	4	6	88	5	5	1
Solvents	93	2	2	3	98	1	1	–
Cocaine	97	1	2	1	94	2	3	1
Heroin	97	1	1	1	97	1	1	1

Drug use among five closest friends

Respondents were also asked to indicate how many of their five closest friends
were regular users of alcohol and tobacco, and how many sometimes used
each of seven types of illicit drug (cannabis and heroin only in the case of YTS
trainees). Table 8.3 shows that the typical respondent had, among her or his
five closest friends, about three or four regular alcohol drinkers, two or three
regular cigarette smokers, and between one and three friends who sometimes
smoked cannabis. The highest rates of alcohol, tobacco and cannabis use
among friends were reported by YTS trainees. But the most unexpected
finding was that the schoolchildren reported consistently higher rates of drug
use among their friends than did the college students (with the exception of
alcohol). However, this difference may have been due to the larger proportions
of working-class young people in the school sample compared with the college
sample, rather than to a higher rate of drug use among Wirral's younger
generation. Furthermore, these differences were marginal, except in the case of
tobacco. Finally, there were also indications that YTS trainees were more
likely to have heroin users among their friends, although over two-thirds of
YTS trainees and over a quarter of the schoolchildren did not answer the
heroin item in the 'friends' question.

Attitudes

The questionnaires were designed to be as brief as possible in order to elicit full
responses to the main questions about drug taking, and so questions about

Table 8.3   Mean number of five closest friends who take drugs

	Schoolchildren	YTS trainees	College students
Alcohol	3.2	4.3	3.9
Tobacco	2.5	2.9	2.0
Cannabis	1.5	2.5	1.4
Mushrooms	0.9	*	0.6
Amphetamines	0.5	*	0.4
LSD	0.5	*	0.4
Solvents	0.4	*	0.1
Cocaine	0.2	*	0.1
Heroin	0.2	0.6	0.2

drug attitudes were not included except for one question in the college students' questionnaire. This asked whether respondents believed that any illegal drugs should be legalised, and if so, which drug(s). The majority of students (63 per cent) thought that no illegal drugs should be legalised, although 58 (26 per cent) believed that one or more illegal drugs should be legalised (12 per cent indicated 'don't know'). Of the 54 pro-legalisation students who gave more information, 87 per cent stated that they thought that only cannabis should be legalised, four believed that cannabis and another drug (amphetamines, LSD or magic mushrooms) should be legalised, two thought that solvents should be legalised, and one believed that all drugs should be legalised.

Relationships between licit drug use, illicit drug use and other factors

Findings were also analysed for evidence of relationships between drug use and other variables. We anticipated that a relationship between drug use and parents' occupational status might be found, though no clear trends were identified. However, associations between drug use and other factors were established.

Area of residence
Consistent variations in the rates of drug use among schoolchildren and college students in different parts of Wirral were identified (see Parker *et al.* 1986c, for details). In the case of schoolchildren, two salient trends were noted. First, pupils attending the two schools in 'high-risk' areas (that is, with catchment areas known to have a high rate of problem drug use and associated social deprivation) exhibited the highest consumption of alcohol, the highest rates of smoking, and a consistently larger number of illicit drug users among their five closest friends. Second, the highest rates of illicit drug trying, regular drug use, and intended drug use were found among youths attending one school in an area of high social deprivation and one school in an area of intermediate social deprivation. Four of the five triers of heroin were attending one school in an area of high social deprivation.
   In the case of college students, the highest rates of illicit drug trying were

found among students resident on the more socially deprived Mersey side of Wirral, notably cannabis and amphetamine trying among Birkenhead and Wallasey students, and experience of psychedelic drugs (LSD and magic mushrooms) among Birkenhead and Bebington students. Deeside students were the only group who had tried neither heroin nor cocaine.

Sex differences

Although, as noted earlier, there were clear differences in the type of alcoholic beverage preferred by males and females, there were few other notable sex differences in alcohol use, apart from a trend towards more frequent drinking among male schoolchildren (only 9 per cent of male pupils drank less than once a month compared with 22 per cent of females). However, females were more likely to smoke cigarettes than their male counterparts: 35 per cent of female pupils and 27 per cent of female students were daily smokers, compared with 26 per cent of male pupils and 20 per cent of male students.

By contrast, males were far more likely to have tried illicit drugs than females: 50 per cent of male pupils and 52 per cent of male students had tried one or more illicit drugs, compared with 26 per cent of female pupils and 34 per cent of female students. Focusing on the most popular illicit drug, 44 per cent of male pupils and 46 per cent of male students had tried cannabis, compared with 24 per cent of female pupils and 31 per cent of female students. Fewer than 6 per cent of female pupils had tried any other illicit drug, compared with 25 per cent of male pupils who had tried magic mushrooms, 24 per cent who had tried solvents, and 12 per cent who had tried amphetamines and LSD. Furthermore, four of the five pupils who had tried heroin were male. However, female students were almost as likely to have tried amphetamines (15 per cent), LSD (9 per cent) and solvents (8 per cent) as male students (18, 13 and 12 per cent respectively), and three of the five students who had tried heroin were female. But magic mushrooms had been tried by 21 per cent of male students compared with 7 per cent of female students.

Males were also far more likely to be regular drug users than females: 14 per cent of male pupils and 17 per cent of male students were regular drug users, compared with 4 per cent of female pupils and 5 per cent of female students. Finally, one in three male students were in favour of legalisation of one or more drugs (typically cannabis), compared with one in five female students.

Past drug use and intended drug use

As might be expected, consistent relationships were also found between past use of illicit drugs and intended use of these drugs. Over 90 per cent of pupils and students intending to try cannabis had already tried it, over 70 per cent of pupils and students planning to try magic mushrooms had already tried them, and between 60 and 70 per cent of those planning to try LSD and amphetamines had already tried these drugs. Only one of the three pupils and one of the three students planning to try heroin had not already tried it.

Focusing on past drug use as an indicator of future drug use, 59 per cent of pupils and 69 per cent of students who had tried cannabis planned to use it again, 55 per cent of pupils and 42 per cent of students who had tried magic mushrooms planned to try them again, 65 per cent of pupils and 39 per cent of students who had tried LSD planned to take it again, and 50 per cent of pupils and students who had tried amphetamines planned to try them again. Two of the five pupils and two of the five students who had tried heroin were planning to use it again in the future. Finally, a maximum of 6 per cent of those respondents who had never tried an illicit drug were intending to use any drug in the future. In short, those young people planning to use illicit drugs were largely those who had already tried them.

Drug use among close friends
A strong and consistent relationship was found between respondents' drug-taking behaviour and that of their five closest friends in each of the three groups of young people. In the case of legal drugs, there was a clear relationship between frequency of drinking and regular alcohol use among close friends. The sharpest difference was between those who drink less than once a week and those who drink more than once a week, the former group having two or three regular drinkers among their close friends, and the latter group having four or five. There was also a strong relationship between smoking status and smoking among close friends, with daily smokers having about twice as many smoking friends as non-smokers (about four compared with two).

Strong associations were also found between respondents' experiences of illicit drugs and the number of their friends who sometimes used these drugs. Those young people who had neither tried nor been offered illicit drugs typically had no friends who had tried drugs. Respondents who had been offered a drug but had not tried it, had, on average, one friend who had tried it in the case of cannabis, magic mushrooms, amphetamines and LSD, but none in the case of the other drugs. By contrast, respondents who had tried an illicit drug had, on average, two or three friends who had tried it in the case of cannabis, about two friends who had tried it in the case of magic mushrooms, amphetamines, LSD or heroin, and about one friend who had tried it in the case of cocaine or solvents.

Licit and illicit drug use
Strong and consistent relationships were also found between smoking and drinking characteristics (frequency, quantity and age of first use) and the use of illicit drugs (trying, regular use and intention to use) in each of the three groups of young people. The full breakdowns are reported in more detail elsewhere (Parker *et al*. 1986c), and will only be briefly summarised here.

The proportion of respondents having tried illicit drugs was clearly related to their frequency of alcohol use. For instance, all of the pupils, three-quarters of the students, and over half of the trainees who drank on most days of the week had tried cannabis, and over a third of respondents who drank once a week had tried cannabis. By contrast, only 10–15 per cent of respondents who drank less than once a week had tried cannabis. Similar correlations were found between frequency of drinking and trying the other illicit drugs. All but one of the 17 heroin triers drank once a week or more often.

The average quantity of alcohol consumed in a 'drinking session' was also clearly related to drug experiences. For instance, the average number of units of alcohol consumed per occasion by non-triers of cannabis was five in the case of pupils and students, and ten in the case of trainees. By contrast, the average number of units of alcohol consumed per occasion by triers of cannabis was nine in the case of pupils, eight in the case of students, and 12 in the case of trainees. In short, cannabis triers were consuming on average an extra three units of alcohol per drinking occasion compared with respondents who had not tried cannabis. Parallel relationships were found between alcohol consumption and the trying of most other illicit drugs.

A third characteristic of drinking which was found to be related to the trying of illicit drugs was age at first use of alcohol. For instance, the typical age at which non-triers of illicit drugs first drank alcohol was 11 years in the case of pupils and 12 years in the case of students. By contrast, the typical age at which triers of illicit drugs first drank alcohol was nine years in the case of pupils and 11 years in the case of students. Heroin triers were found to have typically started drinking one year earlier than non-triers of heroin.

Parallel relationships were found between respondents' smoking characteristics and their use of illicit drugs. For instance, only about one in four non-smokers had tried cannabis (30 per cent of pupils, 19 per cent of trainees, and 20 per cent of students), whereas up to three-quarters of the daily cigarette smokers had tried cannabis (72 per cent of pupils, 53 per cent of trainees, and 72 per cent of students). Similar associations between smoking and trying drugs were found in the case of most other drugs. Only three of the 17 heroin triers were non-smokers (and all three had formerly smoked). Lastly, cigarette smokers who had tried illicit drugs had typically started smoking about one year earlier than smokers who had not tried illicit drugs.

These relationships between the use of legal drugs and the trying of illicit drugs were also apparent with regard to regular drug use and intention to try drugs. In short, early, frequent or 'heavy' drinking and smoking are strong indicators of past, present or future illicit drug use among Wirral's young people.

Drug attitudes and illicit drug use

Finally, the survey data were also examined for evidence of a relationship between pro-drug attitudes and drug-using behaviour, an exercise only possible in the case of college students, who were asked whether they believed that any illegal drugs should be legalised. It was found that 35 per cent of pro-legalisation students were regular drug users (of cannabis in most cases), compared with just 2 per cent of anti-legalisation students. Similarly, 79 per cent of pro-legalisation students had tried cannabis, compared with 24 per cent of anti-legalisation students. The findings were mirrored among triers and non-triers of all illicit drugs.

Summary

This section has reported the findings of three surveys of drug use among almost 700 young people in Wirral during 1986, and may be summarised as follows. The majority of 15–20-year-olds were regular drinkers of alcohol, and most started drinking between the ages of 11 and 14 years. Up to four in ten of these young people smoked cigarettes, and the typical smoker started smoking between the ages of 11 and 13 years. About four in ten of the young people surveyed had also tried illicit drugs: over a third had tried cannabis, about one in seven had tried magic mushrooms, about one in eight had tried amphetamines, and about one in ten had tried solvents and LSD, although fewer than 3 per cent had tried heroin or cocaine. About one in ten young people was a regular drug user, typically smoking cannabis several times a month. Furthermore, for reasons noted earlier in this chapter, the reported rates of illicit drug use were more likely to be underestimates rather than overestimates.

Up to three in ten respondents were intending to use illicit drugs again in the future: over a quarter were intending to use cannabis, and about one in ten were intending to use magic mushrooms and amphetamines. The typical respondent had, among his or her five closest friends, four who were regular alcohol users, two or three who were regular cigarette smokers, one or two cannabis users, and one user of magic mushrooms. One in four students believed that cannabis should be legalised. The main differentiating characteristics of the three groups were heavier drinking and more regular cannabis use among the YTS trainees, and starting drinking and smoking at an earlier age among the fifth-year schoolchildren. Drugs more likely to be used by young people in particular groups included solvents by schoolchildren, and amphetamines by students.

Therefore, assuming that a third of Wirral's 15–20-year-olds have tried cannabis, and given that at least one in ten may be a regular drug user, we can forecast that each 5,000-strong generation of 15–16-year-olds in Wirral may contain over 1,500 cannabis triers and 500 regular drug users. Each generation of drug-using youths is also likely to include 100–200 who will become regular users of heroin.

Finally, clear and consistent relationships were almost invariably found between illicit drug use and such 'indicators' as area of residence, sex, drinking and smoking characteristics (frequency, quantity, age of starting), drug use among close friends, intended drug use, and drug attitudes. Thus, the 'typical' user of illicit drugs in Wirral would be a young male, living in a socially deprived area, regularly drinking and smoking from around the age of 12 years, having two friends also taking illicit drugs, having pro-drug attitudes, and with an interest in experimenting with drugs. Of course, there were also illicit drug users among these young people who had different characteristics from these. Indeed, middle-class users, with stronger attachments to school, and planned careers, are most likely to have falsely denied illicit drug use, and are thus more likely to have been underrepresented.

High time for harm reduction?

Our survey had found that a large minority of 15–20-year-olds in Wirral have experimented with illicit drugs, and that a smaller but substantial minority were regular users. However, the most popular illicit drugs were cannabis, magic mushrooms and amphetamines, with heroin and cocaine being the least popular. Although space limitations preclude a more detailed comparison here, it should be noted that Wirral's young people generally exhibited a higher prevalence of illicit drug use than young people surveyed in other areas of Britain during the first half of the 1980s (see, for example, Mott 1985; NOP Market Research 1982; Plant et al. 1985; Pritchard et al. 1986; RBL 1986; Stuart 1986; Williams 1986). Furthermore, both British and American studies have confirmed the generality of the relationships found in the Wirral research between drug use and other factors, particularly the associations between illicit drug use, smoking and drinking.

Thus, there can be little doubt, given our survey results, that alongside any benefits gained from drug use, there will be a casualty rate amongst this community's young drug-takers. However, the main problems will stem from alcohol- and tobacco-related illnesses and accidents (cf. British Medical Association 1986). It also seems likely that a substantial minority of these young people will begin or continue to use illicit drugs like cannabis, and a much smaller number will, in due course, use heroin. We would suggest that most of these potential heroin users can already be identified on the basis of their earlier, more frequent and 'heavier' use of legal drugs such as alcohol and tobacco, their plans and attitudes concerning drugs, the rate of drug use among their friends and the area in which they live.

Indeed, Kandel (1982) concluded from her important review of 40 longitudinal studies of adolescent drug use that there are discernible stages of drug use which start with tobacco and alcohol use, though she stressed that only a subgroup at each stage are 'vulnerable' to the next stage. The final stages of a full drug career would probably include dependence on heroin and a number of drug-related problems. Kandel (1982, p. 343) advised that 'an important task for clinicians and researchers is to identify that subgroup of youths most at risk for further progression'. The major advantage of this approach is that it would allow us more accurately to target education about drugs at those young people to whom it is most relevant, and who are likely to include most, if not virtually all, of the next generation of problem drug users. This target group could be identified by the presence or absence of such risk 'indicators' as the pattern of legal drug use, friendship networks and area of residence.

However, as discussed in the first section of this chapter, it is now widely acknowledged that school-based primary prevention programmes and mass media anti-drugs campaigns do not achieve their aims of deterring people from drug use, and occasionally have the opposite effect. Consequently, many professionals have begun to argue that the only logical and humanitarian alternative is to target specific groups of 'at-risk' young people for harm-reduction programmes — and sooner rather than later (see, for example,

Carroll 1985; Commonwealth Department of Health 1985; Engs 1981; ISDD 1981; Kay 1986; Dorn 1987; Newcombe 1987a). Indeed, the government's Advisory Council on the Misuse of Drugs begin their report on prevention (Home Office 1984) by stating that 'the increasing incidence of drug misuse casts doubt on the adequacy of existing preventive measures, making it more important than ever to examine their effectiveness and consider ways to improve them or develop better ones' (p. 2). The report then recommends that future prevention policy should focus on two objectives: reducing the risk of an individual engaging in drug misuse; and reducing the harm associated with drug misuse (p. 4).

Harm reduction (also known as 'secondary prevention', 'damage limitation' and 'risk minimisation') involves teaching potential and current drug users all the relevant facts about drugs available to them, and includes three broad categories of instruction: safer methods of drug use (including the relative risks of different drugs), alternative (non-drug) methods of altering mental states, and how to recognise and respond to drug-related problems in oneself and others. In the first case, advice about safe drinking limits, about how to avoid the risk of becoming infected with HIV while injecting heroin (for example, by not sharing needles), and about how to avoid danger when sniffing solvents (for example, by using small plastic bags) are major examples of 'safer use' instruction that have been tried. In the second case, harm reduction involves instruction about various techniques for relaxing or becoming aroused (such as yoga or biofeedback), or about other, more legitimate, activities that are exciting and give 'thrills' (for example, risky sports such as mountain climbing). The third component of harm reduction education involves instruction on identifying drug problems (for example, overdosing) and responding to them (for example, first aid, available drug services).

In short, the emphasis of harm reduction is on controlled use and care rather than abstinence, because its rationale is based on an acceptance of the inevitability of youthful desires to experiment with forbidden or exciting things and activities, and to simply 'get high' (for a more detailed account of the philosophy of harm reduction, see Newcombe 1987a; Weil 1986; and Zinberg 1984). Indeed, there has been an increasing tendency during the last few years for people concerned with drug users to adopt a language and approach which reflects the underlying 'normality' of drug use, including a realisation that 'abstinence is very much out of character with the reality of modern life' (Carroll 1985).

Most advocates of harm-reduction instruction believe that secondary prevention initiatives should complement more general primary prevention measures (see, for example, Home Office 1984, p. 5). Furthermore, there is growing agreement that no drug education programme should be deployed without being scientifically evaluated, whether the objective is to reduce the prevalence of use or the prevalence of harmful use. Policy-makers also need to give greater consideration to how to deal with the complex and/or unforeseen effects of educational interventions, such as an increase in the use of cannabis accompanied by a decrease in the use of heroin, or an increase in the numbers of heroin users in conjunction with a decrease in the number of heroin injectors.

However, though strongly recommended by many professionals working with drug users, the notion of harm reduction education for young people often meets with strong opposition from parents and community groups, whose perspective on drug-taking is understandably based on their emotional attachments to a relative with drug problems, and to the stereotypes of the mass media, rather than to long experience with a variety of drugs users or to the findings of scientific research (see, for example, Pearson *et al.* 1986). Harm-reduction instruction for potential and current drug users would therefore ideally be conducted in tandem with programmes which explained their rationale to parents and other concerned adults. Indeed, this was a key recommendation of one of our research reports presented to the Wirral Drug Abuse Committee. However, this recommendation was ambushed by the confusion and acrimony which has defined the second phase of Wirral's official responses, and which is the subject of Chapter 9.

Wirral's diffidence towards harm reduction was not a peculiar local reaction, though, but rather a typical instance of the built-in resistance among many sections of society to any 'soft' policies which are not geared directly to 'stamping out drug abuse'. This ideological opposition to harm reduction centres around particular social institutions, and is based on several deeply held and interrelated moral beliefs, including the beliefs that using any prohibited drug is inherently irresponsible, dangerous and/or sinful; that alcohol, tobacco and caffeine are justifiable exceptions because they are relatively harmless compared with the prohibited drugs; that heroin is the 'hardest drug', and inexorably leads to addiction, disorder and death; that drug laws prevent drug problems rather than exacerbate them; and, fundamentally, that a harm-reduction approach condones drug use, and would, if implemented, lead to a 'Brave New World' society where drugs control citizens rather than liberate them.

The validity of their objections will be put to the test in the coming decades, as the harm-reduction projects being planned and initiated in Britain and other countries are conducted and evaluated. The outcome of these 'social experiments' will be dependent not only on the behaviour of their subjects, but also on the responses of the wider community to such initiatives. In Wirral, the 'war against drugs' has extended beyond a social conflict between illicit drug users and institutions of social control, to incorporate a new 'civil war' between professionals concerned with drug users. This conflict between advocates of use reduction and advocates of harm reduction is explored in the next, final, chapter.

9

Official responses:
care, control and confusion

In this chapter we will attempt to analyse the way official responses to the heroin 'problem' have developed during the course of the 'epidemic'. The analysis is, however, complicated by three factors. First, our research in and for Wirral is itself part of the local 'official response' and, because of its role, has undoubtedly affected the course of events. There is obviously a problem of objectivity here. Second, changes in official responses are ongoing, making description and analysis quickly obsolete. Third, the actual services in and around Wirral are, like anywhere else, unique and idiosyncratic. Their detail is a product of historical development, funding contingencies, changes in personnel, and so on, and for that reason detailed description is of limited value to the general reader.

For all these reasons we have opted, in this chapter, to keep the accounts of local services fairly brief and instead concentrate on the aims, objectives and ideologies which have underpinned them. This will allow us to get to the essential ingredients which explain why, despite the borough's considerable efforts, official responses, as they have grown, have been beset by confusion and contradiction and why our own research has not been able to offer a range of policy and practice recommendations which dissolve these dilemmas away.

Such difficulties would have been unexpected in 1984 when, as we described in Chapter 1, a multi-disciplinary strategy was developed under the umbrella of an enthusiastic Wirral Drug Abuse Committee. At that time solutions seemed possible, and goodwill and co-operation prevailed. These first-phase responses seemed eminently sensible. First, there was the setting-up of counselling (Drugs Council), treatment services (Detoxification Unit) and rehabilitation facilities (residential hostels) to deal with those already using heroin. Second, there was a clampdown, by the police and courts, on the suppliers and dealers in an attempt to rid the borough's young of doorstep supplies. Third, there were efforts to ensure that young people at risk of taking drugs were 'inoculated' against misuse by introducing a comprehensive health education programme into junior and secondary schools. Finally, the borough also opted to monitor progress and finely tune its responses through detailed research.

Unfortunately, the reality has been very different. With no sign of a large 'outcidence' rate occurring, prevalence remains high and fairly stable. The majority of users are not in regular contact with treatment and counselling services and, although a large number are known to the police and courts, crime remains at an exceptionally high rate. In addition, of course, the arrival of HIV infection has fuelled demands for a re-examination of the whole strategy.

In this chapter we are therefore obliged to outline the relative failure of the Wirral strategy so far. However, as we describe the impact of this programme, it will become apparent that many of the reasons for its lack of success lie beyond the control of the local agencies. We begin by looking at the inability of drugs services to maintain contact and form 'contracts' with the majority of 'problem' heroin users before moving on to the reasons why those charged with orchestrating local official responses have been unable to agree a revised strategy.

In and out of contact

It is difficult to portray the endless movement of problem heroin users in and out of contact with official agencies and programmes. The diagram we offer in this section needs to be envisaged as a hologram or a pinball table in constant motion, so reflecting the flow between the hidden and known drug use sectors, whereby, over the months, users continuously surface and disappear, re-emerge and disappear again. We also need to show that official responses actually affect the hidden–known ratio to the extent that they 'pull' users out of the hidden sector, for instance by prosecuting them for possessing drugs, as well as encouraging them to surface spontaneously by providing meaningful and attractive services. Clearly, persecuting drug users both by heavy policing and refusing to provide user-friendly services, whatever else it achieves, will drive drug use underground (Young 1974), making both the monitoring of drug use and the likelihood of breaking into the smack subculture more remote.

Figure 9.1 is both static and schematic, and is thus no more than an attempt to show what proportion of all heroin users in Wirral have been in and out of contact with official 'services' during the two prevalence periods (which largely correspond with the two phases of official responses). The total user population is based on our known–unknown ratio calculations described in Chapter 5 and we should be clear that on any one day only a proportion of this population will actually use heroin. The number of cases allocated to each agency is complemented by a bracketed figure which identifies cases known

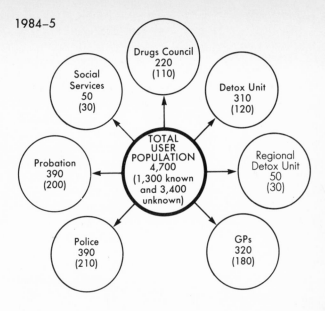

1984–5

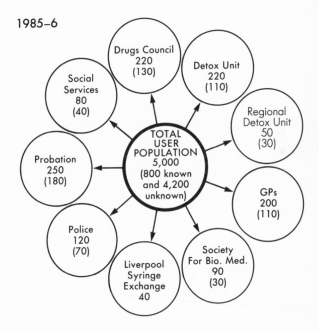

1985–6

Figure 9.1   Changing contact points for 'problem' users 1984–6

uniquely to that agency.[1] This diagram separates statutory 'care and control' agencies, which tend to demand contact, from those agencies offering medical treatment, counselling and other services, which problem users approach more or less voluntarily.

In the first period, the number of cases referred to these treatment and counselling services was about 900, although this only involved about 600 unique individuals. Yet in the second period, with a slight increase in overall prevalence, with a wider range of services available and presumably with a greater awareness among heroin users of the existence of these agencies, the number of cases 'in treatment' went down to about 800, representing about 450 unique individuals. As for statutory agencies (police, probation, social services), in the first period over 800 cases were in their systems whereas in the second period only about 450 cases were known.

In this section we will try to untangle the reasons for these changes, and so explain why a decreasing minority of users are voluntarily 'in treatment' at any one time and why less are being 'captured' by the care and control apparatus.

Medical services

During the first phase, users wishing to seek medical help tended to start with their GP, who either treated them or referred them to the regional or local clinic or both. This was the primary referral circuit. This pattern, although it still survives, has become less used during the second phase both because of the changing attitudes and role of GPs, and the greater knowledge-base users have about the local detoxification regimes.

Between 1983 and 1985 Wirral GPs made over 900 notifications to the Home Office. In 1986 they made only about 100. Given that GPs notify over 85 per cent of Wirral cases, the decline in notifications during 1986 signified either a drop in the number of patients they saw or a new reluctance to notify. Although the latter factor may be partly responsible, we believe that the overriding reason is that GPs are seeing far less heroin 'problem' patients. Whilst this may have something to do with the declining incidence rate, the main reason centres on their disengagement from treating such patients. GPs are another group of professionals who have been left to 'get on with it'. They work alone or in small groups. They rarely co-ordinate their activities or receive special training. Most have never been given any retraining to deal with drug users, and, consequently, even those willing to treat drug users often do so inappropriately or leave themselves open to manipulation by some patients who simply want drugs to be prescribed.

Consequently, GPs have suffered a mixture of 'burn-out' and moral indignation (see also McKegancy and Boddy 1987). As fewer GPs offer users a service so the demand on those doctors who will prescribe increases. This in turn puts intolerable pressure on those remaining doctors who either spontaneously, or because of pressure from partners, withdraw their services from heroin patients. Even the handful of GPs who notified, treated and counselled large numbers of heroin users during the first phase are now withdrawing. As Figure 9.1 shows, the consequence of this is that family doctors are seeing up to a third fewer problem heroin users in the second phase than in the first, a trend which is continuing.

Given the numbers of long-term users in the borough, their personal and social circumstances, and, for many, their increasing ambiguity about continuing heroin use, we might expect there to be a growing demand for treatment in the local Detoxification Unit. This has not been the case. Indeed, since the initial surge of patients during the first year of the Unit's operation and consequent long waiting lists, demand has, at best, been stable, and referrals have in fact had to be encouraged by publicising the service to family doctors and probation officers. The Regional Unit has fared similarly in relation to Wirral patients.

There are several reasons for this. We noted in Chapter 4 that user-patients' perceptions of the Unit's philosophy and regime were rather negative. Patients said they felt the demands and time scale for coming off were unrealistic and the support to help them stay 'clean' insufficient. To this we must add that many users allowed themselves to be referred for detoxification either in an attempt to avoid a custodial sentence from a pending court case, or as part of a 'false' contract with a GP in order to obtain an interim supply of prescribed drugs. These 'unmotivated' referrals, plus the waiting time for an appointment, and the siting of the Unit in a Psychiatry Department, all help explain the high rate of non-attendance for initial clinic appointments and drop-out rate from the Unit's programme. Indeed, the actual numbers of patients in treatment at the Unit is considerably lower than heroin cases 'known' and enumerated in Figure 9.1.

This analysis is not intended as criticism of the Detoxification Unit *per se*. The staff of the Unit are aware of these issues. They believe their detoxification regime, backed by psychological counselling and social work support, is appropriate for those who are genuinely motivated to 'come off'. Their regime is thus unashamedly based on an abstinence model which sees no place for the long-term use of methadone or other substitutes for street heroin. Consequently, the notion of issuing clean needles to patients, except in very special circumstances, is also anathema. Based on their own evaluation, the Unit staff regard a figure of 20 per cent as a realistic success rate in terms of patients who complete their programme remaining drug-free for any length of time.

Statutory care and control

Agencies with generic and statutory responsibilities, like the police, probation service and social services, have all had to respond to the heroin problem as part of their duties. We discussed the role of the police and courts in Chapter 7, noting the far-reaching consequences of their 'clampdown' on the local drugs scene during the 1984–5 period. However, given finite resources and perpetual competition for extra policing between areas and across crime categories, this particular exercise had to come to an end. It should also be said that the police were beginning to rethink their strategy with a view to using a 'softer' approach and linking into other kinds of 'services'. The net result of this was a reduction in prosecutions, and thus a drop in the number of heroin users known to probation officers. However, other processes at work in hiding heroin use from probation also need to be discussed because they relate to the amount of help and advice heroin user-offenders can receive from the service.

Throughout its history, the probation service has had to live with a dual care and control function. The academic (for example, Raynor 1985) and practice literature (Walker and Beaumont 1981) is built on this duality and the dilemmas it causes practitioners. Given the low success rate of official responses in relation to reforming offenders, whether custodial or community-based, and the probation service's belief that social-work skills must also play a part in the criminal justice system, the addition of heroin dependency into the frame has not been welcome. In retrospect, the fate of Wirral's three dozen or so probation officers has been little better than that of their user-offender clients. Both have been left adrift for several years. User-offenders, as we have shown, have been shunted in and out of penal institutions. Probation officers for their part have been left to 'get on with it', armed only with their individual skills. They have thus picked up caseloads consisting, on average, of 25–30 per cent heroin user-offenders, and in some cases over 50 per cent. They have also, in the absence of any overall strategy, become highly reactive and 'ground down' by the continual pressures of workload, unreliable clients and punitive courts. Officers have thus on their own admission developed a deeply negative attitude to drug user-offenders (Adams and Buckett 1987). Consequently, their professional ethos, to prevent custody wherever possible and provide the courts with alternatives to custody, has been sorely stretched. In the face of such anomie their tendency has been to let the courts get on with 'sending down' all but the most 'deserving' heroin offenders.

In 1987, however, and as a fairly direct response to the research findings outlined in Chapter 7, the probation service reviewed its 'traditional' response and, after a detailed in-house examination of more innovative and pro-active possibilities, appointed two drugs-liaison officers. Their role has been to provide a specialist assessment procedure for drug user-offenders, to offer support to main-grade officers and to attempt to utilise community-based services in the region more effectively. The new strategy also involves providing a post-custody rehabilitation programme in an attempt to help ex-prisoners, usually drug-free on release, to remain so, by providing them with housing, employment and counselling services. This is to be achieved by greater co-operation and co-ordination with other agencies such as voluntary housing associations and employment projects, and formal referrals to the new 'second phase' residential-rehabilitation facilities.

Although the success of such a strategy will inevitably be limited, it does provide a much more rational approach to the use of resources. It also offers probation officers themselves greater support and opportunity to plan more realistic programmes with and for their clients. Ironically, however, the success of such an initiative for the offenders 'new to crime' and those who have not yet received a custodial sentence is likely to be undermined by wider processes. The great difficulty for statutory social workers and probation officers at this stage of the 'epidemic' is that heroin users are increasingly reluctant to tell, to expose their identity. They are aware of the consequences of such an admission.

In 1982, when user-offenders began to enter the court system, local probation officers, defence solicitors and magistrates were confronted with a new phenomenon. Initially, solicitors would use heroin addiction as a plea of mitigation. They would assure the court that their client would never normally be involved in such a serious crime as a domestic burglary and that he or she only behaved so badly as a result of a heroin habit. He or she needed help. Very quickly, however, local courts, alarmed by the growing numbers of user-offenders and the rocketing crime rate, took a very harsh line. They tended to regard a heroin-using acquisitive crime offender as a 'custody case', commenting in open court that 'the public had to be protected', that heroin users would continue to commit crime, that custody would 'cure them of their addiction'.

After some three years of this approach, user-offenders, unsurprisingly, have become extremely reluctant to reveal their drug taking to the courts, and hence to their solicitor and probation officer. This strategy of not telling, along with the diminishing returns from saturation policing in relation to the local drugs scene, largely explains the reduction in the number of problem heroin users probation officers know about (see Figure 9.1). There is considerable irony in this situation given that, to some extent, the police and the courts, themselves perplexed that custody does not cure, are beginning to take a more flexible approach to dealing with problem user-offenders and that the probation service is trying to provide more support and treatment options. So, at a time when the early identification of heroin use amongst offenders, particularly those new to crime, is being attempted in order to provide services, the presence and willingness of offender-users to identify themselves is in decline.

Statutory child care

It was clear from the first prevalence survey that the Borough of Wirral's Social Services Department did not know many problem heroin users. Few young people perceive these departments as places of help which can be turned to without hesitation. Adolescents regard social workers as part of the 'authority' system: social workers are linked with the courts, they can take children into care, and so must be viewed with suspicion (Parker et al. 1981). Both workers and their potential clients are aware of these issues and tensions. Consequently, the heroin cases known to social workers during the first phase tended to result from their knowing the family for another reason, and because of related statutory responsibilities. This preoccupation with statutory duties is a role increasingly thrust upon social services, particularly in hard-pressed areas like Merseyside.

We have referred repeatedly to the fact that female heroin users are more likely than males to remain in the hidden sector. They commit less crime and so are at less risk of being caught by the police and fed into the courts system, and even when they are 'busted' by the police, particularly for dealing along with a male partner, the woman is often not arrested, with her boyfriend or cohabitee 'taking the rap' instead, particularly if the couple have children.[2] However, there is a vital exception to this, and that concerns the one aspect of womanhood which forces female users to surface — pregnancy. Between the beginning of 1982 and the end of 1985, 25 babies were born in the local hospital's maternity unit to women who were smokers of heroin at some stage of their pregnancy. Many, having not had regular menstrual periods for over a year as a consequence of heroin use, were not aware of their pregnancy until quite late in their term. All this was exceptional enough and of considerable interest to the medical profession (Klenka 1986). Then, during 1986 and into 1987, the rate of new heroin-maternity cases rocketed, and no less than 32 babies were born to the same number of women during a 15-month period. Thus, when most other agencies were seeing a fall in the number of contacts with problem users, maternity-unit doctors, nurses and social workers were experiencing an unprecedented increase in such problematic cases. The need to call case discussions and case conferences and institute care proceedings under child-care legislation grew as a consequence. Most of these women were not previously known to social and health service staff as heroin users.

The nurses, doctors and hospital social workers 'picking up' these cases were fully aware that many of the women went to considerable lengths to conceal their heroin use. The patients would refuse to see a social worker or try to undermine the results of a urine test by bringing someone else's sample. They were fearful that their baby would be taken from them. These tactics correspond with what female users in our interview sample told us about their fears.

Clearly, there will be occasions when the compulsory removal of a baby or child from its heroin-using mother may be deemed necessary and both statutory agencies and expectant mothers have been made only too aware of this by much-publicised cases (Berkshire 1985). In fact, only a small minority of Wirral's 90 or so cases have led to adoptions, statutory care orders and separation of mother and child. Nevertheless, these cases remain closely monitored with supervision orders, 'at-risk register' reviews and regular visits from social workers being routine.

Here, then, is another quite major consequence of the heroin epidemic and the classic example of both the female users and the local state's care and control dilemma. Becoming pregnant provided a major motivation for most of these women to come to the surface, to 'come off', if only temporarily, and obtain proper ante-natal care. Yet they went through this process, through the examinations and the awkward interviews, fearing that the official response would be to take their baby from them and heap moral disgrace upon them. For the social services, the dilemma rests on the very meaning of heroin use. Case law as yet remains ambiguous about whether continued heroin use during pregnancy is itself a reason for taking statutory child-care proceedings. This ambiguity, plus the pressure to play safe due to the welter of public enquiries which have castigated social workers for leaving children in the care of 'inadequate' parents (Corby 1987), encourages the trend to 'case-conference' every child-care case involving heroin. This very process of bringing together a plethora of professionals to review the 'risk' itself brings a symbolic meaning to heroin use which is not repeated for other drugs such as alcohol, with its infamous track record in relation to foetal damage and domestic violence. We will return to this issue of the meaning of heroin use at the end of the chapter.

Counselling and residential services

Opening in spring 1984, the Drugs Council was an essential part of the first-phase strategy. We noted in Chapter 4 that the clients of this service regarded it fairly positively. Furthermore, the number of referrals to the Drugs Council has remained stable since it opened. The voluntary and totally confidential nature of the service and its client-centred approach appear to be the vital components in the agency's ability to maintain contact and form 'contracts' with users.

The Drugs Council employs a team leader, six counsellors and several support staff. Although it provides general drugs information and a telephone service, it is predominantly a counselling agency. Client services are of three types. First, nearly all new clients undertake an assessment programme utilising groupwork methods. This programme aims to help new clients explore their options within the community, encourage personal responsibility for addiction and help sort out pressing medical and social problems, as part of a move towards a more stable lifestyle. Following induction, clients will either undertake a placement in a nearby linked residential unit or begin a programme of counselling, either individually or in a structured group. The nature of the groups changes through time but tends to focus on life skills, relaxation, anxiety management, or support for drug-free clients. Clearly the reality of working with 'problem' drug users means that these programmes must be flexible. Clients may not turn up for appointments or alternatively turn up at another time. Some clients will not be ready to give up drugs and must instead be encouraged to explore their feelings and relationship with drugs.

Although staff turnover has been low amongst Drugs Council employees, there has been a high rate of sick leave. In part this has been due to the nature of the task, but much of the occupational stress suffered has been a result of the source and level of funding. Resourced by time-limited grants from central government, the Drugs Council has throughout its history had to struggle first with accommodation difficulties and then with overload because additional staff could not be funded.

A further difficulty faced by the Drugs Council staff relates back to our discussion about the disengagement of GPs from treating drug users. This has made it much more difficult for counsellors to arrange medication and treatment in conjunction with their counselling programmes.

On the other hand, the arrival in 1987 of two new residential facilities, one local and one regional, has provided the counsellors and other professionals who act as referral agents with a vital additional therapeutic tool. The need for a local residential facility linked with the Drugs Council was long planned. However, because of the need to find appropriate property, arrange its conversion into a hostel via a housing association, and recruit staff, this facility actually emerged during the second phase. This bedsit hostel takes younger adults of both sexes and will accept referrals from outside the borough to fill its 14 beds. Its nine staff run a very strict and highly structured programme which can last up to six months. Residents must be drug- and alcohol-free, except for tobacco use. They must undertake urine tests and detected drug use is likely to lead to their expulsion. Leaving the premises without authority or breaking any of a battery of rules can also lead to removal, although those asked to leave can return to try again after an interval. The hostel runs very much as a therapeutic community using residents as human resources and decision-makers and relying on intensive small-group activities and exercises to work on personal and social skills and methods of coping with craving and temptation to reuse drugs.

At the time of writing, a second regionally organised residential facility run by Phoenix House was just opening. This new facility will also tend to run as a therapeutic community catering for long-stay drug-free residents.

Alternative services

Electro-Acupuncture

The Society of Biophysical Medicine enquired about the setting up of a service in Wirral in 1985, but, having received little encouragement from the local authority and covert hostility from the medical fraternity, opened up in the city of Liverpool instead.

The Electro-Acupuncture Centre offers treatment using small electrical currents which are passed into the body via surface electrodes on the toes or fingers. This stimulation theoretically leads to the body creating endorphins, morphine-like substances, which act as a substitute for heroin. The treatment is thus intended to aid withdrawal and to offer a natural substitute to heroin. In other words, it is an alternative form of detoxification, but one based on natural substances and normal body processes. The treatment requires patients to attend every day for between a week and three months, but with 14 days being the average.

The success of this therapy is still to be proven, but what is important from our point of view is that the Centre has been able to attract a large number of patients and lock into 'natural' user and parent networks. Most volunteer helpers are parents or former users. The Centre has no waiting lists, and it opens seven days a week from 10a.m. to 7p.m. It provides an informal and confidential service. Users know they will not be notified to the Home Office or have their names referred to, for example, the police. In its first year the Centre had nearly 600 patients. Over a quarter of the first 300 were from

Wirral. Many of these were our 'new users' who travelled out of the borough people 'get off' than 'stay off'. Consequently they attempt to help their clients

The Centre staff accept that their treatment is more successful at helping people 'get off' than 'stay off'. Consequently they attempt to help their clients with accommodation, education and housing problems and also welcome back those who have relapsed.

Methadone maintenance and Syringe Exchange Scheme
Although strictly medical services, the two approaches described here were not available in Wirral at the time of writing and so are regarded as 'alternatives'. In 1985 the city of Liverpool opened a Drug Dependency Unit. The Unit quickly became established as one of the busiest in the country. The psychiatrist in charge is an advocate of methadone maintenance for users who cannot or do not intend to become drug-free. Consequently, although offering a wide range of services, the Unit has become known for its 'liberal' prescribing policy. Amid some considerable confusion about whether this Unit had regional status or not, a stream of referrals and requests for maintenance from Wirral users was received. These referrals, although not often taken up by the city clinic, were certainly quoted by some as 'evidence' to support the view that such a facility should be available in Wirral — a suggestion not welcomed by the long-standing Regional Clinic or Wirral's Detoxification Unit. The presence of two very different treatment approaches just a few miles apart, and a good deal of media interest in the debate,[3] have led to the politics of heroin becoming a very lively issue.

More fuel was added in late 1986, when next door to the city clinic, a Syringe Exchange Scheme was opened. The Exchange was primarily a response to the fear of HIV infection being spread amongst and from the local injecting population. The new facility, with its open-door approach, attracted both publicity and a large number of injectors. It quickly built up over 500 customers in six months, about 80 of whom travelled from Wirral. Furthermore, these genuinely voluntary customers of the Syringe Exchange service were obviously users with 'problems', having been using 'dirty works', and often showing signs of physical damage due to inept injecting techniques. Once again, therefore, it was illustrated that an 'attractive' user-friendly service could bring users, not otherwise in contact with services, to the surface.

These two alternative services not only formally linked the heroin and AIDS agendas together, but opened up the debate about harm-reduction and drug-free lifestyles.

Prevention in schools

We reported in Chapter 8 on the relatively high levels of alcohol, tobacco and cannabis usage amongst fifth-formers in some of the Borough of Wirral's schools. Whilst not strictly a service for drug users, the borough's strategy for health education must still be regarded as part of the official response to heroin. Indeed, it was agreed right from the outset that a cornerstone of the strategy to 'fight drugs' must be prevention. The rationale of the prevention argument is that children, probably the younger the better, must be educated about all harmful substances, and must grow up to understand the dangers associated with their use and abuse. If schoolchildren, supported by the schools and properly informed parents, can internalise a mature and responsible outlook to drugs and harmful substances then they will have been 'inoculated' against temptation and the self-destructive behaviour often associated with abuse.

Wirral's Education Department worked with great commitment between 1984 and 1987 to set this long-term strategy in place, whilst at the same time accepting that, in the short run at least, drug abuse would still arise in some of their secondary schools and have to be dealt with. The Department built on responses discussed in Chapter 1 so that by 1987 its health education pack for nine- to 11-year-olds had become a national model (TACADE 1986). The pack, made up of background information, slides and teaching material, encourages a broad-based approach to health education. There are components for teachers, pupils and parents. The pack looks at danger in the home, school and environment. It shows how a very wide range of chemicals and drugs can be hazardous and focuses in particular on the dangers to health of alcohol and tobacco. It tries to avoid stimulating new interest in illicit drugs amongst this young age group.

Although not properly evaluated, initial responses to the programme were obtained from parents, head teachers and teaching staff, and subsequently published (Amos 1986). The general feeling to emerge was that the programme was a 'good thing' and should be continued and further developed. Interestingly, the Department has devoted as much attention to expanding its programme into the younger age group as the older. Consequently, although advisers and co-ordinators have been appointed to extend this sort of programme into the borough's 26 state secondary schools, as much effort has been made with infant and nursery units. In 1986 a pack was introduced into all nursery schools and schools with nursery classes, and in 1987, a photo-pack for five- to -seven-year-olds was launched. The wisdom of such a strategy will be put to the test in the coming decade.

The politics of official responses

The attractiveness and user-friendliness of official responses seem vital if we regard making and sustaining contacts with problem heroin users as the prerequisite for helping them and, in the last analysis, their community. We have implied that client-centred services clearly attract the most positive responses. The 'success' of the Drugs Council, the Electro-Acupuncture Centre and the Syringe Exchange Scheme are based on these principles. All these agencies offer confidentiality and a non-judgemental approach. They are all services which are accessible and need not be approached through a third party. None is connected with the Home Office Notifications Index.

Being part of the legal apparatus undoubtedly makes doctors, psychiatrists, probation officers and social workers 'suspect' and suspicious. Furthermore, the vast majority of these local state professionals did not volunteer to work with drug users, nor have they been trained to do so. Like the users themselves, they have been placed in a situation about which they have doubts, difficulties and, as we shall discuss in the next section, moral reservations. Ironically, therefore, many of those charged with making official responses are also unhappy about the circumstances in which they meet with users. The new users believe that the Notifications Index is not confidential; they believe that social workers may take their children from them; they believe that disclosing a heroin habit to their probation officer will worsen their position in court; they believe that most GPs are unhelpful. They are right to believe this. There are good reasons why a decreasing minority of users make themselves known to certain agencies.

A crisis of confidence

Faced with the fact that the heroin problem was not going away but was instead developing in a number of 'unfortunate' ways, the Wirral Drug Abuse Committee talked itself into a kind of collective paralysis during 1986. It could agree nothing, not even the minutes of the previous meeting. Its long debates saw the membership breaking up into unlikely alliances and turning more and more to deeply felt moral perspectives to arrive at certain conclusions.

The situation was further complicated by the changing national and regional mechanisms for financing and developing drugs services. Wirral, frustrated in 1984 by the failure of the Regional Health Authority to help it develop services, turned to its local-authority-controlled financial structures, notably the Department of Environment's Inner Area Programme. This was highly productive for developing first-phase services. However, slowly but surely, nationally and regionally, drugs services have become financed and managed by 'health' structures. A symbol of this change, created by the increasingly influential role of the Regional Health Authority, was the demand that Wirral, as a District Health Authority, set up a District Drug Dependency Problem Team. This 'officer' committee of health and local authority managers and professionals working within drugs services came into being at the beginning of 1987. It brought together many who were already senior members of the Drug Abuse Committee but also introduced some new actors onto the scene such as psychiatrists with deeply opposing views about the role of methadone! Consequently this committee immediately recreated the acrimony already taking place in the Drug Abuse Committee. Wirral thus went into 1987 with the guardians of its 'official responses' caught between two administrative and funding structures and with two decision-making committees both equally unable to reach any substantive agreement about how to respond to the continuing adverse effects of widespread heroin use.

In attempting to explain this crisis in the management and development of the borough's drugs service, it is very tempting to offer the reader transcripts of these meetings and cameos of how some of the more bizarre suggestions, made by certain members, were arrived at. They were all there: the chain-smoking councillor who banged his packet of cigarettes on the table in opposition to providing 'safe usage' education to heroin users, before going off to the members' bar for a few pints to help him drive home; the GP who wanted to cut off drug users' hands; and the senior social work manager who believed that if people wouldn't heed the warnings and give up drug-taking spontaneously, then it would be better to let them die rather than give them clean needles. This would in the end, however, miss the point, for the crisis which these decision-making structures faced was essentially a crisis of confidence. There are good reasons why these experienced politicians and professionals, normally successful managers in their own organisations, floundered in multi-disciplinary settings created to deal with responding to drug misuse. However, to pull these issues out we need to step back from the local situation and use a more analytic approach. We must explore the beliefs and prejudices which are at the heart of the disagreement about official responses. First, we must look at the arguments presented for and against methadone maintenance and the provision of clean syringes for injectors, before exploring more fundamental and often only privately expounded beliefs about the compatibility of preventive as opposed to harm-reducing philosophies in health education, and the moral worth of heroin users. This moral 'baggage' people carry with them influences their perspective on the care and control debate, on whether heroin addicts are victims or culprits and whether they deserve help or not. It is 'baggage' because it is not a coherent set of ideas and beliefs and because, as yet, it is often not articulated in public.

Maintenance and needles

The dilemmas surrounding the use of methadone to maintain heroin users are well rehearsed within psychiatry (see *Druglink* 1987) but have only recently, because of the enormous scale of heroin use, become the subject of public debate. The picture which has emerged suggests that psychiatry is at civil war over the issue. The message received by decision-makers at a local level is thus unclear. Whom are they to believe, the psychiatrist on their left or the one on their right?

The doctor on their left is part of the pro-maintenance lobby, he is a 'new realist'. His perspective is presented with confidence and commitment. It argues that, faced with the scale of the problem, the socio-economic profile of the new generation of heroin users, and the fact that despite all the risks and official warnings these users continue in their habit, maintenance and clean needle exchanges become essential weapons in damage limitation. The thesis has at least four points:

1 There is growing evidence that these new users finance their habit through almost daily crime. This crime is damaging the community's social solidarity and producing great harm to the victims of robbery, burglary and theft. Maintenance would reduce drug-related crime by providing free drugs to the addict.
2 The cycle of heroin dependency and crime of these new users is very hard to break. The economic and social costs in terms of policing, prosecution and

prison, as well as child care and probation services, are enormous. Maintenance seems likely to reduce these costs.

3 Prescribing drugs helps keep users with otherwise dangerous and 'chaotic' lifestyles more stable and reduces their need to commit crime and fraternise with the 'smack subculture'. It brings them into contact with services which can monitor their drug use and crime and move them towards a drug-free existence in years to come as they mature out of the heroin lifestyle.

4 Oral and self-injectable maintenance provides these users with clean drugs and equipment, so reducing the risk of contracting diseases, particularly HIV infection. Drug injectors are the key group in the spread of HIV infection to the heterosexual population. The consequences of needle-sharing in Scotland have been devastating. Maintenance is becoming a public health issue, and the spectre of AIDS means that the reservations and objections of prohibitionists must be set aside for the public good.

This perspective can in fact be taken further to include the prescribing of heroin and other controlled drugs, or the introduction of a smokeable substitute for street heroin, given the unattractiveness of oral methadone for many heroin smokers.

The psychiatrist on the right finds such arguments unconvincing. He points to history. Maintenance has been tried and found wanting. The 1984 government guidelines discouraging maintenance are sensible and based on clinical experience. Maintaining is fraught with dangers:

1 It condones or endorses unnecessary and health-damaging drug use. It sends a double message when operated alongside detoxification regimes.

2 It weakens a patient's ability to move towards living a drug-free life. Maintained users have a 'narcotics prop' which they lean on when under stress instead of developing more appropriate problem-solving techniques.

3 It is very difficult to draw up criteria about who should and should not be maintained. Maintained patients can become a management problem as they remain 'live' cases which keep out-patient clinics under constant pressure, perhaps deflecting resources from detoxification and treatment regimes.

4 Maintaining large numbers of patients can be very stressful for the doctor or psychiatrist, particularly if he has moral or ethical doubts about the practice.

5 Maintained users may try to get over-generous prescriptions and sell their methadone on the black market. The drug may then cause problems for someone else. Also there is no guarantee that maintained users will not continue to use street heroin or other drugs in conjunction with their prescribed methadone.

To a large extent the 'clean needles' debate follows the methadone discourse, since, on the one hand, maintenance often requires the supplying of clean equipment, and, on the other, the provision of clean syringes does beg the question 'shouldn't customers be given clean drugs to put in them?'. However, the two 'services' can be run independently, and setting up a clean syringe exchange scheme in areas with a high prevalence of heroin use, even without accompanying prescribing, can be supported for the following reasons. First, in terms of the spread of disease and HIV infection, we cannot afford not to provide a syringe exchange scheme in areas where heroin use is prevalent (Parry 1987). This is because in such areas not only is there a hard core of daily injectors but a significant minority of casual or occasional injectors who are likely to share syringes and needles with other injectors. Second, such a scheme brings users into contact with services, often for the first time. It is vital that these users, who may have their own health problems and be putting others at risk, are 'monitored' and offered professional advice rather than left in the hidden sector.

Not surprisingly, this compromise is unacceptable to those 'abstentionists' who want to see hard drugs disappear from the scene altogether. For them, such a service is an admission of defeat. It implies that injecting is safe, so encouraging both new drug use and a switch from smoking to injecting. Furthermore, despite the clean-for-dirty exchange principle, it is likely that such a scheme will increase the supply of needles 'loose' in the community. Discarded equipment will become a new form of street litter to be picked up by young children. Finally, such a scheme will cause outrage amongst parents, who will lose faith in officialdom.

Those opposed to a syringe exchange scheme in Wirral routinely made these points and even when the setting up of such a scheme became inevitable they quickly distanced themselves and their agencies from such a service, making sure it was sited and managed a long way from their own sphere of influence.

Prevention is better than no cure

These disagreements about the form of the Borough of Wirral's second-phase strategy went deeper than the specific pros and cons of any particular service. They stemmed from more deep-seated beliefs about how to respond to the heroin situation. Those who opposed maintenance and syringe exchange were also likely to reject all harm-reduction initiatives in favour of preventive health education. Consequently, the senior education officials responsible for the schools and youth service, in opposing any suggestion that instruction in the safe usage of illicit drugs should be given in these facilities (even in the face of the results reported in Chapter 8), would find allies amongst those opposing maintenance and clean needles for the borough. This alliance to oppose harm-reduction or damage-limitation exercises is based on the belief that prevention is better than cure. For those committed to abstinence and prohibition in relation to illicit drugs such as cannabis and heroin, any compromises in the 'war against drugs' are unacceptable. Compromise and concession cannot be accepted because that is how 'the battle' will be lost. Safe drug use is a nonsense and thus talk of using illicit drugs safely sends a double message to 'our children' and so sabotages preventive health education programmes. For the prohibitionists, not only is prevention better than cure but it is, in the long run, infinitely better than no cure. For that is what the 'warriors' believe the new realists have to offer — no cure and unacceptable concessions in the war against drugs and the moral degeneration of society's young. This stance, often punctuated with strong moral judgements, had considerable force in a community like Wirral. It transcended the community's class differences, for instance, by linking highly-paid 'conservative' professionals with the self-help groups from the borough's poorest and most heroin-affected townships. Here, working-class parents with heroin-using children have formed their own support groups around similar notions of prohibition. They understandably want their children to be drug-free. The thought of their sons and daughters sitting in the bedroom injecting free drugs with clean needles is anathema to them.

The new realists attack the warriors of abstention and prohibition on several fronts. They point to the research evidence which documents the dismal failure of preventive programmes. New school-based schemes will suffer the same fate because drug use is normalised in our society and indeed, in terms of alcohol and tobacco, actively promoted through advertising and sponsorship. They accuse the preventive lobby of hypocrisy for taking a weak and woolly line over these licit drugs, despite their health-damaging effects, whilst condemning other potentially harmful drugs such as cannabis. They suggest this hypocrisy stems from moral prejudice and an inability to transcend repressive drugs legislation and view the situation objectively and realistically. They believe that people take drugs because they are pleasurable and potentially helpful. However, all drug taking carries a risk, be it alcohol or heroin. What is required is instruction in the safer usage of all these drugs and consistency in their promotion and control. Finally, the 'new realists' suggest that those committed to prevention and prohibition are willing to sacrifice the present generation of determined drug-takers. This abandonment is unacceptable to the 'new realists' who insist that official responses must include reaching out to those many thousands of determined users who are and will continue to be unmoved by preventive programmes. Reducing harm by teaching about and aiding safer drug use is an inescapable commitment, therefore.

The prohibitionists and the new realists, because of their deep ideological commitments, were not always in agreement that the two approaches could be amalgamated into a revised strategy for the borough. Many felt obliged to insist that the two philosophies were inherently incompatible. Their disagreements, and the confusion created, explain why progress was so slow and the politics of official responses so bitter.

Why should such polarisation occur amongst these local decision-makers? Yet again we must dig deeper, for in the end the credibility and acceptability of either of these perspectives is determined by each person's position in a moral spectrum regarding drug use in general and heroin use in particular. At one end of the continuum we have the abstentionists who ideally and genuinely want a drug-free society. At the other end we have those who believe that we should have a 'free drugs' society. The latter believe that citizens should be able to use whatever substances they like as long as this does not cause harm to others. At various points along the continuum between we have mediators who position themselves according to their more disparate or uncommitted views about drug use and the heroin 'problem'. What those at both extremes do agree about is that most of their opponents are culture-blinded into viewing alcohol and tobacco as safe.

In Wirral, parents' groups and Education Department officials would place themselves towards the 'drugs-free' pole in relation to illicit drugs yet would regard alcohol and tobacco more liberally. Whilst individual professional positions will be unique, we can also place types of service response along the continuum. Thus, user-centred services such as the Drugs Council and those officials backing a flexible approach to prescribing and provision of syringes because of the need for pragmatic non-judgemental official response, will hold the middle ground. Beyond them, we have those overtly supporting flexible prescribing and syringe exchange as a necessary harm-reduction strategy, but who would ideally like to see a complete revision of society's attitudes to drug use and an accompanying change in the law. For them the heroin problem is not about the drug itself but about official responses to its use. They have, to a large extent, used the AIDS agenda as a vehicle to move the debate about drugs towards a more libertarian position. We noted in Chapters 4 and 6 that many users would ally themselves with this position.

Finally, we should be clear that this analysis of the ideological and moral underpinnings of the heroin debate is not readily available to these local actors. The structures they work in and the way that district health and local authority committee meetings and the agendas operate discourages formal talk of fundamental value systems in favour of concrete detail. Consequently the psychiatrists, policemen, education officials, councillors, administrators and the rest would often not recognise their contributions as stemming from any specific theoretical or ideological perspective which is shaped by moral and cultural rule-systems. They would prefer to view their ideas as the product of organisational and professional experience and 'just knowing' when something is right or wrong.

Deskilled by heroin

All this is reported not to deride these local decision-makers but to explain why developing coherent responses to heroin is so difficult. It is at the local level, in areas like Merseyside, amongst the consequences of mass unemployment, urban decline, and financial constraints on service development, that the problem of dealing with heroin's side-effects comes home to roost. It is at the local level, not in the offices of far-away government ministers, that the dilemmas of accepting simultaneous primary prevention and harm-reduction advertising campaigns have to be worked through.

Heroin has in many ways deskilled these local decision-makers. They have had to accept that the endless hours of committee talk have not produced solutions. The pace of the drugs scene and the arrival of AIDS have unsettled them and consequently, because fundamental moral positions cannot be overtly or routinely used, they have increasingly had to fall back on common sense to get through. There has also been a tendency to try to fend off responsibility for any new or controversial initiatives. These tactics lead to the unpacking of the heroin baggage referred to earlier. This baggage is tipped onto the table and passed around. Consequently 'my department' really means 'me'; 'this Council will not tolerate' loses the additional 'if I have anything to do with it'; 'we have done all we possibly can' really means 'and I'm not going to get involved in trying anything else'.

Here, then, is another hidden cost of the borough's heroin problem. It has deskilled and disillusioned a wide range of mainly, public sector workers. GPs have been manipulated and pressured by problem heroin users and many have withdrawn their services. Probation officers have become reactive and disillusioned with user-offender clients. Drugs counsellors have struggled with burn-out and occupational illness, and, finally, local decision-makers on the borough's two drugs committees have lost their way.

Notes

1 These figures are estimates based on our multi-agency survey data.
2 We are not suggesting that women receive preferential treatment in this official response to females and motherhood. Indeed this policy places enormous responsibility on the woman who has to cope with financial and domestic rearrangements, prison visiting and often the demand from user-customers for a continuation of any heroin business. Furthermore if she has been reliant on her husband to 'score', difficulties in obtaining her supplies will also occur.
3 *World in Action*, May 1987, and *Newsnight*, August 1987, for instance.

Postscript: the story so far

'Living with Heroin: The Sequel' will probably never emerge, given the pain associated with writing this book. Clearly, it should be written, for the story is far from over. We are painfully aware that the Wirral scene, like drugs scenes elsewhere, is constantly changing. Even as we complete this book we know that the move towards injecting is continuing, that drugs other than heroin are starting to be injected by new users, that even the few family doctors who have offered a limited prescribing service to users are withdrawing, burnt out by the enormous demand. There are also signs that the financial gains to be made in the heroin distribution system are bringing a violent edge to 'the business'.

The impasse in official responses, described in the last chapter, is beginning to be broken. This is not because the local actors have changed their moral minds but because the trends we have documented, in terms of the consequences for the community of not reaching out to current users, make 'doing nothing' politically untenable.

Obviously we have no neat solutions for this community. There is no heroin solution as such, just a series of 'unattractive alternatives' (see Parker and Chadwick 1987) with which to try to manage the epidemic and its unwanted consequences. At the heart of this strategy must be a realisation that flexibility and pragmatism are not signs of weakness, and an understanding that the way our society perceives and responds to heroin is as important as the effect of the drug itself.

Bibliography

Adams, D. and Buckett, T. (1987). *Drugs Misuse in Wirral: A Probation Service Response,* Merseyside Probation Service, mimeo.

Amos, F. (1986). *An Evaluation of the Wirral Primary Schools Drug Prevention Initiative,* Wirral Education Authority.

Auld, J. *et al.* (1986). 'Irregular work, irregular pleasures: heroin in to 1980s' in R. Matthews and J. Young (eds), *Confronting Crime,* Sage, London, Chapter 8.

Barker, D.J. and Rose, G. (1979). *Epidemiology in Medical Practice,* Churchill Livingstone, Edinburgh.

Becker, H. (1963). *Outsiders: Studies in the Sociology of Deviance,* Free Press, New York.

Belle, D. and Goldman, N. (1980). 'Patterns of diagnoses received by men and women' in Guttentag *et al.* (1980), pp. 21–30.

Bennett, T. and Wright, R. (1986a). 'The impact of prescribing on the crimes of opioid users', *British Journal of Addiction,* vol. 81, pp. 265–73.

(1986b). 'The drug-taking careers of opioid users', *The Howard Journal,* vol. 25, no. 1 pp. 1–12.

Bertaux-Wiame, I. (1979). 'The life-history approach to the study of internal migration', *Oral History,* vol. 7, no. 1.

Box, S. (1987). *Recession, Crime and Punishment,* Macmillan, London.

Brake, M. (1980). *The Sociology of Youth Culture and Youth Subcultures,* Routledge and Kegan Paul, London.

British Medical Association (1986). *Comparative Mortality from Drugs of Addiction,* British Medical Association, London.

British Medical Journal (1985). 'Media drug campaigns may be worse than a waste of money', *BMJ,* vol. 290, p. 416.

Burr, A. (1987). 'Chasing the dragon: Heroin misuse, delinquency and crime in the context of South London culture' (unpublished).

Cameron, D. and Jones, I. (1985). 'An epidemiological and sociological analysis of the use of alcohol, tobacco and other drugs of solace', *Community Medicine,* vol. 7, pp. 18–29.

Carroll, R.J. (1985). *Shifting Gears: Making Secondary Prevention Strategies Primary in the Substance Abuse Field,* Eagleville Hospital, Eagleville, Pennsylvania.

Cohen, S. (1973). *Folk Devils and Moral Panics,* Paladin, London.
Commonwealth Department of Health (1985). *Drug Education Programmes in Australia,* National Drug Education Committee, Canberra.
Corby, B. (1987). *Working with Child Abuse,* Open University Press, Milton Keynes.
De Alceron, R. (1969). 'The spread of heroin in a community', *Bulletin on Narcotics,* July–September, pp. 17–22.
Ditton, J. (1977). *Part-Time Crime,* Macmillan, London.
Donaghoe, M. *et al.* (1987). 'How Families and Communities Respond to Heroin', in Dorn and South (1987a).
Dorn, N. (1981). 'Social analyses of drugs in health education and the media' in C. Busch and S. Edwards (eds), *Drug Problems in Britain,* Academic Press, London. (1987). 'Minimization of harm: a U-curve theory', *Druglink,* vol. 2, pp. 14–15.
Dorn, N. and South, N. (1983). *Of Males and Markets,* Research Paper No. 1, Centre for Occupational and Community Research, Middlesex Polytechnic. (1983–4). 'Youth, Family and the Regulation of the Informal', *Resources for Feminist Research,* 12, Dec/Jan. (1985). *Helping Drug Users,* Gower, Aldershot. (1987). *A Land Fit for Heroin?,* Macmillan, London.
Dorn, N. *et al.* (1987). *The Limits of Informal Surveillance,* ISDD, London.
Druglink (1987). Vol 2, 4, pp. 10–14.
Elliott, D. *et al.* (1983). 'The prevalence and incidence of delinquent behaviour, 1976–80', The National Youth Survey Project Report No. 26 (Behavioural Research Institute, Boulder, CO).
Engs, R.C. (1981). 'Teaching responsible drug and alcohol use' in L.R. Drew *et al.* (eds) *Man, Drugs and Society: Current Perspectives,* Proceedings of the First Pan-Pacific Conference on Drugs and Alcohol, Canberra, Australia.
Feldman, H. (1968). 'Ideological supports to becoming and remaining a heroin addict', *Journal of Health and Social Behaviour,* vol. 9, pp. 131–9.
Fraser, M. and Hawkins, J. (1984). 'Social network analysis and drug misuse', *Social Service Review,* March, pp. 81–97.
Frith, S. (1984). *The Sociology of Youth,* Causeway Books, Ormskirk.
Fry, L. (1985). 'Drug abuse and crime in a Swedish birth cohort', *British Journal of Criminology,* vol. 25, no. 1, pp. 46–59.
Gandossy, R. *et al.* (1980). *Drugs and Crime: A Survey and Analysis of the Literature,* US Department of Justice, Washington, DC.
Gay, M. *et al.* (1985). *The Interim Report: Avon Drug Abuse Monitoring Project*; Hartcliffe Health Centre, Bristol.
Glaser, B. and Strauss, A. (1967). *The Discovery of Grounded Theory*, Aldine, Chicago.
Greenberg, S. and Adler, F. (1974). 'Crime and Addiction', *Contemporary Drug Problems,* vol. 3.
Guttentag, M., Salasin, S. and Belle D. (eds) (1980). *The Mental Health of Women,* Academic Press, New York.
Hall, S. *et al.* (1978). *Policing the Crisis,* Macmillan, London.
Hammersley, R. and Morrison, V. (1987). 'Effects of polydrug use on the criminal activities of heroin users', *British Journal of Addiction,* vol. 82.
Hanson, B. *et al.* (1985). *Life with Heroin,* Lexington Books, Lexington, MA.
Hartnoll, R. *et al.* (1985a). *Drug Problems: Assessing Local Needs,* Drug Indicators Project, London.
Hartnoll, R. *et al.* (1985b). 'Estimating the prevalence of opioid dependence', *The Lancet,* 26 January, pp. 203–5.

Haw, S. (1985). *Drug Problems in Greater Glasgow,* SCODA, Glasgow.
Henige, D. (1982). *Oral Historiography,* Longman, London.
Home Office (1984). *Prevention,* HMSO, London.
   (1985a). *Criminal Careers of those born in 1953, 1958 and 1963,* Statistical Bulletin.
   (1985b). *Statistics of the Misuse of Drugs in the United Kingdom,* HMSO, London.
   (1986). *Statistics of the Misuse of Drugs in the United Kingdom,* HMSO, London.
Hughes, P. (1977). *Behind the Wall of Respect,* University of Chicago Press, Chicago.
Hunt, L.G. and Chambers, C.D. (1976). *The Heroin Epidemics: A Study of Heroin Use in the United States,* Spectrum, New York.
ISDD (1981). *Teaching about a Volatile Situation,* Institute for the Study of Drug Dependence, London.
Jameson, A., Glanz, A. and MacGregor, S. (1984). *Dealing with Drug Misuse: Crisis Intervention in the City,* Tavistock, London.
Johnson, B. *et al.* (1985). *Taking Care of Business,* Lexington Books, Lexington, MA.
Kandel, D.B. (1982). Epidemiological and psychological perspectives on adolescent drug use. Journal of the American Academy of Child Psychiatry, 21, 328–47.
Kay, L. (1986). 'Prevention charter', *Druglink,* vol. 1, no. 2, pp. 10–11.
Klenka, H. (1986). 'Babies born in a district general hospital to mothers taking heroin', *British Medical Journal,* vol. 293, pp. 745–6.
Knoke, D. and Kuklinski, J. (1982). *Network Analysis,* Sage, London.
Levy, B. (1985). *Prevalence of Abuse of Substances in the Brighton Area Health Authority,* Drug Dependency Clinic, Brighton.
McBride, D. and McCoy, C. (1981). 'Crime and drug-using behaviour', *Criminology,* vol. 19, pp. 281–302.
McKegancy, P. and Boddy, F. (1987). *Drug Abuse in Glasgow,* University of Glasgow, mimeo.
Malyon, T. (1986). 'Full tilt towards a no-win "Vietnam" war on drugs', *New Statesman,* 17 October 1986, pp. 7–10.
Merseyside Police (1987). *Report of the Chief Constable for the Year 1986.*
Mitchell, J.C. (1969). *Social Networks in Urban Situations,* Manchester University Press, Manchester.
Moss, A.R. (1987). 'AIDS and intravenous drug use: the real heterosexual epidemic', *British Medical Journal,* vol. 294, pp. 389–90.
Mott, J. (1985). 'Self-reported cannabis use in Great Britain in 1981', *British Journal of Addiction,* vol. 80, pp. 37–43.
   (1986). 'Opioid use and burglary', *British Journal of Addiction,* vol. 81, pp. 671–7.
Mott, J. and Taylor, M. (1974). *Delinquency Amongst Opiate Users,* Home Office Research Study no. 23, HMSO, London.
Muncie, J. (1984). *The Trouble with Kids Today,* Hutchinson, London.
Newcombe, R.D. (1987a). 'High time for harm reduction', *Druglink,* vol. 2, pp. 10–11.
   (1987b). 'The Liverpool Syringe Exchange Scheme for drug injectors: a preliminary report', *Mersey Drugs Journal,* vol. 1, no. 1, pp. 8–10.
NOP Market Research (1982). *Survey of Drug Use in the 15–21 Age Group undertaken for the* Daily Mail, National Opinion Polls, London.
Palombi, F. (ed) (1984). *Combating Drug Abuse and Related Crime,* United Nations Social Defence Research Institute, Rome.
Parker, H. *et al.* (1981). *Receiving Juvenile Justice,* Blackwell, Oxford.

Parker, H., Bakx, K. and Newcombe, R. (1986a). *Drug Misuse in Wirral: A Study of Eighteen Hundred Problem Drug Users Known to Official Agencies,* University of Liverpool, Department of Social Work Studies, mimeo.

(1986b). 'Heroin and Crime: The Impact of Heroin Use on the Rate of Acquisitive Crime and the Offending Behaviour of Young Drug Users', University of Liverpool, Department of Social Work Studies, mimeo.

(1986c). *Alcohol, Tobacco and Illicit Drug Use among Young People in Wirral,* University of Liverpool, Department of Social Work Studies, mimeo.

(1987). *Wirral's Heroin Future,* University of Liverpool, Department of Social Work Studies, mimeo.

Parker, H. and Chadwick, C. (1987). *Unattractive Alternatives: Dilemmas for Drugs Services in Wirral,* University of Liverpool, Department of Social Work Studies, mimeo.

Parker, H. and Newcombe, R. (1987). 'Heroin use and acquisitive crime in an English community', *British Journal of Sociology,* vol. 38, no. 3, pp. 331–50.

Parry, A. (1987). 'Needle Swop in Merseyside', *Druglink,* vol. 2, p. 7.

Pattison, C.J., Barnes, E. A. and Thorley, A. (1982). *South Tyneside Drug Prevalence and Indicators Study,* Centre for Alcohol and Drug Studies, St Nicholas Hospital, Newcastle upon Tyne, mimeo.

Pearson, G. (1986). 'Heroin and Diversity', *Drug Questions,* vol. 2, pp. 3–5.

(1987). *The New Heroin Users,* Blackwell, Oxford.

Pearson, G., Gilman, M. and McIver, S. (1986). *Young People and Heroin: An Examination of Heroin Use in the North of England,* Health Education Council, London.

Peck, D.F. and Plant, M.A. (1986). 'Unemployment and illegal drug use: concordant evidence from a prospective study and national trends', *British Medical Journal,* vol. 293, pp. 929–32.

Plant, M.A. (1975). *Drugtakers in an English Town,* Tavistock, London.

Plant, M. (1986). 'Heroin campaigns screw it up', *Times Educational Supplement,* no. 3604, p. 25.

Plant, M.A., Peck, D.F. and Samuel, E. (1985). *Alcohol, Drugs and School-leavers,* Tavistock, London.

Polley, S., Tober, G. and Raistrick, D. (1986). *Drug Survey, 1985–86,* Addiction Unit, Leeds, mimeo.

Preble, E. and Casey, J. (1969). 'Taking care of business', *International Journal of Addiction,* vol. 4, no. 1, pp. 1–24.

Pritchard, C., Fielding, M., Choudry, N., Cox, M. and Diamond, I. (1986). 'Incidence of drug and solvent abuse in "normal" fourth and fifth year comprehensive school children: some socio-behavioural characteristics', *British Journal of Social Work,* vol. 16, pp. 341–51.

Raynor, P. (1985). *Social Work, Justice and Control,* Blackwell, Oxford.

RBL (1986). *Heroin Misuse Campaign Evaluation: Report of Findings,* Research Bureau Limited, London.

Richman, A. and Abbey, H. (1977). 'Heroin epidemics: facts and artifacts', *Proceedings of the 39th Annual Scientific Meeting of the Committee on Problems of Drug Dependence,* July 1977, pp. 504–30. National Research Council, Washington, D.C.

Robertson, J.R. *et al.* (1986). 'Epidemic of AIDS related virus (HTLV–III/LAV)', *British Medical Journal,* vol. 292, pp. 527–9.

Rosenbaum, M. (1981). *Women on Heroin,* Rutgers University Press, New Brunswick, New Jersey.

Rutherford, A. (1986). *Growing Out of Crime,* Penguin, Harmondsworth.

Spear, H.B. (1969). 'The growth of heroin addiction in the U.K.', *British Journal of Addiction,* vol. 64, pp. 245–55.

Stephens, R. (1972). 'The truthfulness of addict respondents in research projects', *International Journal of the Addictions,* vol. 7, pp. 549–58.

Stewart, T. (1987). *The Heroin Users,* Pandora Press, London.

Stimson, G.V. and Oppenheimer, E. (1982). *Heroin Addiction: Treatment and Control in Britain,* Tavistock, London.

Stuart, P. (1986). 'Solvents and schoolchildren — knowledge and experimentation among a group of young people aged 11 to 18', *Health Education Journal,* vol. 45, pp. 84–6.

Swadi, H. and Zeitlin, H. (1987) 'Drug education to schoolchildren: does it really work?', *British Journal of Addiction,* vol. 82, pp. 741–6.

TACADE (1986). *Health Education: Drugs and the Primary School Child* (educational pack), Salford, Teachers' Advisory Council on Alcohol and Drug Education.

Trebach, A.S. (1982). *The Heroin Solution,* Yale University, New Haven, CT.

Walker, H. and Beaumont, B. (1981). *Probation Work,* Blackwell, Oxford.

Watson, P. (1984). 'The fate of drug addicts on a waiting list', Prestwich Hospital, Manchester, mimeo.

Weil, A. (1986). *The Natural Mind,* (revised edition), Jonathan Cape, London.

Whittaker, B. (1986). *The Global Connection,* Jonathan Cape, London.

Whyte, W.F. (1943). *Street Corner Society,* University of Chicago Press, Chicago.

Williams, M. (1986). 'The Thatcher generation', *New Society,* 21 February, pp. 312–15.

Young, J. (1974). 'Mass media, drugs, and deviance' in P. Rock and M. McIntosh (eds), *Deviance and Social Control,* Tavistock, London.

Zinberg, N. (1984). *Drug, Set and Setting: The Basis for Controlled Intoxicant Use,* Yale University Press, New Haven, CT.

Index